M · E · D · L · E · Y

OF

FIRST NATIONS COOKING

Creating a Family Heirloom

Unusual   Interactive   CookBook

Ross & Linda Maracle

Tyendinaga Mohawks

Medley of First Nations Cooking

by
Ross & Linda Maracle

Copyright 2003.

"Top of Totem Native Crafts"
P. O. Box 292
Deseronto, Ontario K0K 1X0

Email
rossmaracle@spiritalive.org

Special Notes
The flowered designs on the corners of each recipe
represent the beadwork of the Woodlands First Nations Peoples.
Design Layout: Lois Brough   **Proof Reader:** Elsie Ward

Giving Kudos

Create A CookBook That Becomes A Family Heirloom

After all these years of cooking and many times hearing, "Mom, can I have that recipe?" I thought how tremendous it would be to put together a CookBook that would become a Family Heirloom. What you have in your hands is what I wished I had had in my cookbooks throughout the years.

"SPECIAL AND UNIQUE INTERACTIVE FEATURES" . . .

- **"Food Fun Fotos"** - space for Your favourite photos
- **"My Comments"** - place at the end of each recipe for Your comments
- **"Favourite Recipes"** - space for recipes collected from family & friends
- **"Selected Menus for Special Occasions"**

Winning at the Mohawk Fair

Some of these recipes have become part of our traditional family heirloom. Take for instance, the peanut butter cookie recipe. My son Ross, used it twenty years ago at the Mohawk Fair, and won. Just this past year at the same County Fair, my grandson, Dakota, won also. The baking tradition lives on!

I am mother to three children, grandmother to eight grandchildren and two sons-in-law, many of these recipes have been "family taste tested" with "Wow! the apple pie is fantastic!" to "I can't believe the Harvest Chowder is so incredibly tasty!" to "What's missing in the turkey dressing?"

Rich Heritage

I have wonderful memories of my childhood watching my mother, as she busily worked around the kitchen. I would be so enraptured by the method of her preparation and the fragrances that filled the kitchen. My love of cooking came from her desire to make things taste good and her delight when she saw that people appreciated her cooking.

A great enjoyment that I have in cooking is that it is a continuation of my mother's joy. Many of these recipes are a collection of savoy and unusual recipes gathered from family and friends over the past 37 years.

My desire is that this Cookbook will bring present enjoyment, but will also become a rich heritage of your comments on food and cooking that will become a personalized **"Treasured Family Heirloom!"**

Enjoying the Joy of Cooking,

Linda Maracle

Tyendinaga Territory, Deseronto, Ontario

Unforgettable Memories

As you begin browsing through the pages of this book, we trust that the recipes will stir memories and take you back to a time before frozen foods and pre-packaged meals.

To those special times of Christmases past, when unforgettable fragrances filled the house ~ of a turkey roasting or fresh bread being baked in the oven.

To those unforgettable memories at your Aunt's or Grandmother's house; of soft and warm chocolate chip cookies just out of the oven, or the anticipation of having a slice of the best apple pie in the world.

Even now, the aroma of sliced apples bathed and luxuriously simmering in butter, cinnamon and brown sugar, covered with a flaky crust dusted with sugar, fills your mind and stirs your tastebuds.

GET READY TO BE COMPLIMENTED

Whatever the case, you have before you a CookBook that can help you warmly touch the lives of people by preparing an unforgettable meal or giving a gift of some delectable dessert that you have personally prepared.

These recipes reflect the diversity of our Nation: from the "Quick Salmon RollUps" of the Haida in B.C. To the "Crabby Delights" of the Mic:maq of Nova Scotia; to the "Indian Corn Soup" of the Iroquois and to the "Bannock" of the Ojibwa and Cree.

Go ahead! Have fun with the recipes. In this age of hustle and bustle Take The Leap!!! Surprise Yourself, set aside time each week and let **"Special Food Creations"** *become the enjoyable new hobby of your life!*

The Other Half!
Ross Maracle

The Menu

Selected Menus
for Special Occasions

Your Additional Favourite Recipes

At the end of each section there are two
pages to write in or paste on Recipes from
family members and friends.

The Gallery of . . .

Favourite "Food Fun Fotos"
Pages Eighty-Nine and Ninety

Note from My Husband

Congratulations Sweetheart! Your amazing creativity in cooking over the last 37 years is finally coming to print. I have always admired you for your unflappable ingenuity in cooking for either a handful or for hundreds at campmeetings or conventions. It has always been with a personal touch.

When on limited budgets throughout the years, you have responded to healthy appetites, providing tasty and nutritious meals with resourcefulness, I admire you!

"Medley of First Nations Cooking" is a reflection of your hospitality and the beautiful meals that you have enhanced with natural accents and served to our guests over the years. This book carries the same spirit of excellence with practical ideas and inspiring recipes.

Thank you Linda for appointing me as your "Official Co-Author." I have enjoyed every minute of designing this cookbook with you. My deep gratitude also goes out to our children, who were our "Editorial Committee": Rachel, Rebecca and Ross for their suggestions and to our grandchildren who are our "Official Taste Testers."

I will be forever grateful Linda for allowing me to include my well-worn jokes that you say are no longer funny, under the "Lighter Fare." I can hardly wait to receive the first letter that states, "If only for the jokes alone, the cost of buying 'Medley of First Nations Cooking,' was worth it!"

Last, but not least, I want to on our behalf, honour and express our deep appreciation to "Our Creator" for blessing us with the ideas for this Cookbook.
Nia:wen! Miigwetch!

Forever,
Your Favourite
Fan!
Ross

Amazing Appetizers

Sweet Corn Bannock

with Cinnamon Honey Butter

3 cups Flour	3 tbsp. Shortening	2 tbsp. Cinnamon
½ tsp. Salt	½ cup Water	1 ½ cups Honey
1 tsp. Baking Powder	½ of 19 oz. can Creamed Corn	1 lb. Butter, softened

Mix together flour, salt and baking powder. Then add one at a time, shortening, water and corn, stirring gently to incorporate. Shape into 1" balls and deep fry in oil until brown. Drain on paper towels.

In a processor mix butter and cinnamon, slowly drizzle in honey on medium speed. Mix well.

Put 2 balls on a wooden skewer or large toothpick and drizzle honey butter over and serve. Makes 24.

Occasion _____ Date _____
Comments _____
_____
_____
_____

Lighter Fare   My Grandma started walking five miles a day when she was sixty-five. Today she's eighty and I don't know where in the world she is!

Quick Smoked Salmon Roll-Ups

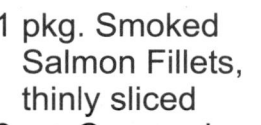

1 pkg. Smoked
  Salmon Fillets,
  thinly sliced
8 oz. Cream cheese
1 bunch dill weed

2 tbsp. Mayonnaise
Salt & Pepper to taste
1 tsp. Lemon juice
1/4 tsp. Garlic, minced
Toothpicks

Lay out fillet, cut into strips about 1" X 3". Mix together remaining ingredients except dill weed.

Spread small amount on salmon piece and roll up with sprig of dill showing. Hold together with a festive toothpick.

Refrigerate until ready to serve. Serves 40. Recommended: two per person. Serve on crackers.

Occasion _____ Date _____

Comments _____

_____

_____

Salmon Cheese Ball

7 3/4 oz. Red Salmon
3 oz. Cream Cheese,
  softened
1 tsp. Lemon juice
1/2 tsp. prepared
  Horseradish

1 tsp. Grated Onion
Salt to taste
1/4 cup Parsley,
  minced
1/4 cup Pecans,
  chopped fine

Mix salmon, cream cheese, lemon juice, horseradish, onion and salt. Refrigerate until firm. Form into a ball and roll in mixture of parsley and nuts.

Occasion _____ Date _____

Comments _____

_____

_____

Helpful Hint Thaw fish in milk. The milk draws out the frozen taste and provides a fresh-caught flavour.

Gingered Chicken Pot Poppers

3 cups finely
   shredded cabbage
1 egg white, lightly
   beaten
1 tsp. Soy Sauce
1/4 tsp. Crushed
   Red pepper
1 tbsp. minced
   fresh Ginger

1 tbsp. Oyster sauce
½ tsp. Honey
1 tbsp. Peanut oil
4 green Onions with
   tops finely chopped
4 lbs. ground Chicken
   breast, cooked and
   drained

24 Won Ton
   Wrappers
Cornstarch
½ cup Water
1/8 tsp. crushed
   Red pepper
2 tsp. grated
   Lemon Peel

Steam cabbage 5 minutes. Cool. Take out excess moisture and set aside.

Filling: Combine egg white, soy sauce, 1/4 tsp. Red pepper, ginger and green onions in large bowl. Stir in cooled cabbage and chicken. Spread out and fill won tons with 1 tbsp. filling per wrap. Gather all edges into a bundle and twist to close. Place Pot Poppers on large baking sheet, dust with cornstarch. Refrigerate 1 hour.

Prepare sauce with remaining ingredients, except oil, in a small bowl. Set aside.

Heat oil and cook on sheet at 400F. until bottoms are golden brown. Keep on a cookie sheet and pour sauce over top cooking 3 more minutes, covered, at 400F. Uncover and cook until liquid is gone. Serve warm.

Serves 8 to 10.

Occasion _____ Date _____
Comments _____
_____
_____

⚠ Tip   On cold winter days, soups are ideal for casual get-togethers. Borrow 3 or 4 slow cookers and fill each with a different soup, stew or chowder, or better yet, ask friends to bring their favourite soup.

Mohawk Scone Pizza

1 cup rinsed and
   drained Cannellini
   Beans
2 tsp. Lemon juice
2 med. Garlic cloves,
   minced
2 X 8" flat Scones

2 tsp. Olive oil
½ cup seeded
   Tomtoes, chopped
½ cup red Onion
1/4 cup Feta Cheese,
   crumbled
2 tbsp. Pitted Black
   Olives

Preheat oven to 450F.

Place beans in bowl and mash with fork. Stir in lemon juice and garlic.

Arrange Mohawk fry bread scones on baking sheet. Brush top with oil, and bake 6 minutes.

Spread bean mixture evenly on scones. Arrange remaining ingredients on scones. Bake for 10 minutes.

Cut in quarters . Serve hot.

Occasion _____ Date _____
Comments _____
_____
_____

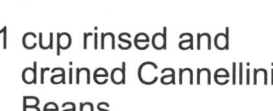

Lighter Fare At a funeral, a friend was giving a eulogy. He said, "My friend John's gone. This is just his old body. It's like the parable of the walnut: 'The shell's here, but the nut's gone!'"

Lemon Pepper Dandelion Delights

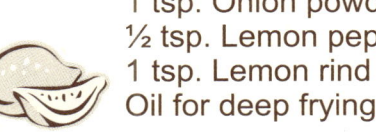

3 cups Buttermilk
  Pancake mix
½ tsp. Herb & garlic
  seasoning
2/3 cup Milk
2 cups fresh finely chopped Dandelion greens

1 tsp. Onion powder
½ tsp. Lemon pepper
1 tsp. Lemon rind
Oil for deep frying

    Combine pancake mix and seasonings together. Stir in milk and mix well.   Add dandelion greens, stirring just enough to hold together. Drop by teaspoon into hot oil ~ 375F. Cook until golden brown.

    Drain on paper towels. Serve hot with honey mustard or just plain. Good cold too!

Occasion _____ Date _____

Comments _____

_____

Garlic Ginger Chicken Strips

4 skinless, boneless
  Chicken pieces (1lb.)
1/4 cup Soy sauce
1/4 cup Vinegar
1 tbsp. Fresh Basil
6-8 cloves Garlic, minced

½ tsp. Crushed Red
  Pepper
2 tbsp. Honey
1 tsp. Ginger
½ tsp. Pepper
1/4 tsp. 5-Spice Powder

    Cut chicken breasts into 4 lengthwise strips. Combine soy sauce, vinegar, basil, garlic, honey, ginger, pepper, crushed pepper. Add chicken strips and coat. Cover and marinate for 30 minutes at room temperature.

    Drain chicken, reserve marinade. Grill or broil chicken. To serve, transfer to platter. Add toothpicks. Makes 16.

Occasion _____ Date _____
Comments _____

_____

Helpful Hint *A few drops of lemon juice added to whipping cream helps it whip faster and better.*

Crabby Delights

2/3 cup Cream
   Cheese, softened
2 tsp. Lemon juice
1 tsp. Hot Pepper
   Sauce
1 pkg. Crabmeat

1/3 cup chopped
   Red pepper
2 green Onions,
   chopped all
64 Cucumber slices
   for low fat, or
   Melba toast rounds

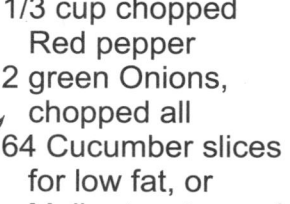

Combine well cream cheese, lemon juice and hot sauce in medium bowl. Stir in crabmeat, pepper and onion. Cover and chill until ready to serve ~ 1 hour at least.

When ready to serve, top crab mixture on each round.

Occasion _____ Date _____
Comments _____
_____
_____

Stuffed Cherry Tomatoes

15 Cherry tomatoes
½ cup Cottage Cheese
1 thinly sliced
   Green Onion
1 tsp. Parsley, chopped

½ tsp. snipped
   fresh Dill
1/8 tsp. Lemon
   Pepper

Cut thin slice off bottom of each tomato. Scoop out pulp; invert tomatoes on paper towel to drain. Combine cottage cheese, green onion, parsley, dill and lemon pepper. Spoon into tomato. Serve at once.

Refrigerate ~ good for 8 hours.

Occasion _____ Date _____
Comments _____
_____
_____

⚠ Tip   If there is a bake sale, try this. Offer a sample plate for those who can't decide. Place on it a couple of cookies, piece of fudge, slice of cake, etc.

Savoury Cream Puffs
and Mushroom Filling

4 tbsp. Butter
½ cup Flour
2 eggs, room
   temperature
1/4 cup finely chopped
   fresh Sage

} Make earlier same
day of serving.

Preheat oven to 375F. Combine ½ cup water and the butter in saucepan. Bring to a boil. Remove and add flour all at once, stirring vigorously with a wooden spoon. Return to medium heat and stir until flour leaves side of pan and forms a ball. Remove and cool for 5 minutes.

Add eggs, one at a time beating hard until dough is smooth. Place large rounded tablespoon on ungreased cookie sheet 2" apart. Bake for 30 minutes or until brown. Carefully cut in half, scoop out centres and cool.

Filling: ½ onion, finely
4 tbsp. Butter   chopped
Salt & Pepper   1 lb. Mushrooms,
                                   finely chopped

Mix butter and onion and cook over medium heat for 2 minutes. Add mushrooms, stirring occasionally until all water is gone. Season and let cool.

Helpful Hint If you look like your passport photo, then you probably need to try out this recipe!

Wild Rice Cheese Balls

1 qt. Water
2 cups Wild rice,
   washed
2 eggs

1 cup grated
   Cheddar Cheese
1 cup dried bread
   crumbs
Oil for frying

Boil water and as boiling slowly add washed wild rice in a stream so water never stops boiling. Stir once or twice, reduce heat to slow, simmer and cover for 35 minutes. Remove from heat and drain through a sieve. Drain thoroughly.

In a large bowl, beat eggs lightly. Add rice and stir with fork lightly. Set aside.

Cut cheese in ½"cubes. Take 2 tbsp. of rice mix and cover, forming into ball. Roll in breadcrumbs (season if you like) and place on waxed paper tray in refrigerator for 45 minutes.

Heat fat to 375F. and fry balls 8 minutes or until golden brown. Drain on paper. Serve immediately or reheat in microwave for 10 minutes.

Cranberry Jelly is a good sauce for dipping.

Occasion _____ Date _____
Comments _____
_____
_____
_____

Lighter Fare Why did the man stare at the can of orange juice? Because it said, "Concentrate."

Fantastic Fungus

4 medium Portabello Mushrooms, cleaned
1 lb. Fresh Snails, cooked & shelled (canned can be used)
1/8 cup chopped Chives
4 Cloves, minced

8 tbsp. Butter
2 tbsp. Balsalmic Vinegar
1 cup smoked Gouda Cheese, shredded
½ Lemon wedge
1/8 cup chopped Parsley
Salt & Pepper to taste

Clean mushrooms, remove gills and stems (saved for stock). With a melon baller, make 6 pockets (try not to go through back of mushroom) for snails.

Saute mushroom tops in 2 tbsp. Butter until partially cooked.   Set aside.

In a frying pan, combine 2 tbsp. butter, garlic, salt, pepper, 2 tbsp. gills, balsalmic vinegar, ½ of chives and ½ of parsley. Saute 3 minutes.

Place mushrooms on cooking sheet, put a snail in each pocket, drizzle with remaining melted butter mixture, squeeze lemon juice over all.   Cover liberally with cheese and put under broiler until bubbly and brown.   Serve hot. Garnish with remaining parsley and chives.

Ross, Jr.'s favourite creation!

Occasion _____ Date _____

Comments _____

_____

_____

_____

 Tip There is no death, only a change of worlds.
- Chief Seattle

Amazing Appetizers

Favourite Recipes from Family Members and Friends

(Recipes can be written in or pasted on)

Amazing Appetizers

Favourite Recipes from Family Members and Friends

(Recipes can be written in or pasted on)

A
M
A
Z
I
N
G

A
P
P
E
T
I
Z
E
R
S

Breads & Spreads

Cheese & Dandelion Pate and Spread

1 cup Cracker Crumbs
4-5 cups crushed
   and chopped
   Dandelion Greens
½ cup Spinach, chopped
1/4 tsp. ground Nutmeg
½ cup plain Yoghurt

3 tbsp. Parmesan Cheese
4 egg whites
1 small Onion, chopped
1/4 tsp. Paprika
3/4 cup Cottage Cheese
1/4 cup toasted Sesame
   Seeds

Steam together dandelion greens and spinach until tender (2 to 3 minutes). Put in saucepan and continue cooking until liquid is gone. Lightly squeeze any remaining liquid out.

In a medium bowl, combine greens, remaining ingredients... then add cracker crumbs.

Spray a loaf pan and pour in mixture. Bake at 350F. for 45 - 60 minutes. Check at 45 minutes.

Serve warm with crackers to spread on. Serves 8 - 10 people.

Occasion _____ Date _____
Comments _____
_____
_____
_____

⚠ Tip   Make a real family tree by planting a tree for someone special every year. In Autumn there are terrific sales at garden centres . . . the perfect time to shop and plant.

Bruschetta a la Dande

16 slices crusty
   Italian Bread
2 cloves Garlic
1/4 cup Olive Oil
6 Garlic Cloves,
   mashed to paste
Salt and Pepper to taste

½ cup coarse Salt
2 tbsp. Oil
6 cups Dandelion
   Greens
½ cup chopped
   Gruyere Cheese

Brown bread slices under griller until brown on both sides. Rub toast with garlic on one side; then brush same side with oil. Set aside.

In large skillet on low heat, cook garlic paste in oil stirring for 1 minute. Add greens and salt and pepper, and saute on moderately high heat, stirring tenderly for 3 minutes. Pour off liquid. Put greens aside to cool slightly. Sprinkle cheese on greens. Mound greens on oiled side of toast. Serve warm.

Serves 16.

Occasion _____ Date _____
Comments _____
_____
_____

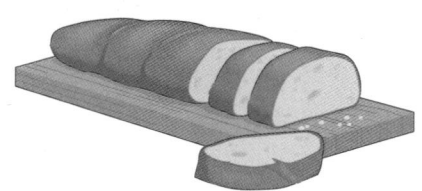

Lighter Fare A preacher demonstrating the ills of whiskey, took a worm and dropped it in a glass of whiskey, whereby it sank to the bottom dead. "What does this prove?" he said. An old codger yelled out in a slightly blurry voice, "Well preacher, it proves if you drink whiskey, you won't have worms!"

Tyendinaga Tea Cake

2 cups + 2 tbsp. brewed
   Tyendinaga tea
1 cup Raisins
2 ½ cups Flour
1 cup Sugar
½ tsp. Butter

2 tsp. Baking powder
1 tsp. Salt
1 tsp. Cinnamon
1/4 tsp. Cloves
1/4 tsp. Black Pepper
6 tbsp. Icing sugar, sifted

Preheat oven to 350F. Pour 2 cups hot tea over raisins and soak.

In bowl, sift flour, sugar, baking powder, salt and spices. Cut in butter and blend thoroughly.

Add tea with raisins and stir until smooth. Pour into loaf pan and bake 50 - 60 minutes.   Allow to cool 10 minutes and remove loaf from pan.

Stir together 2 tablespoons tea and icing sugar and brush over loaf.

Occasion _____ Date _____

Comments _____

Indian Summer Cornbread

1 1/4 cups yellow Cornmeal
½ cup Flour, sifted
1 tbsp. Baking powder
1 tsp. Salt
1 medium can Creamed Corn

½ tsp. Baking Soda
1 Egg, beaten
1 1/4 cups Buttermilk
1/4 cup Shortening,
   melted

Sift together cornmeal, flour, sugar, baking powder, salt and baking soda. Mix together creamed corn, egg and buttermilk. Quickly stir dry ingredients and shortening into milk and egg mixture, leaving a few lumps.

Pour into 8" square greased pan. Batter will be thin.

Bake at 425F. for 15 - 20 minutes or until nicely browned. Cool and cut into squares. Serves 6 - 8 people.

Occasion _____ Date _____

Comments _____

Helpful Hint When baking, use medium to large eggs; extra large eggs may cause cakes to fall when cooled.

Mohawk Corn Bread

2 cups cooked (white flour corn) Corn Kernels
1 tbsp. Cornflour
2 cups Kidney Beans, drained & dried
Salt to taste

Add enough water to all of above ingredients to make a sticky dough. Shape with hands into flat cakes about 4" round and 1" thick.

Drop into a pot of boiling water (6 cups). They will sink to the bottom, rising to the top when they're done. Remove, drain and let dry and cool.

Slice up and fry in a tablespoon of butter, salt and pepper to taste, until brown and crispy on each side. Serve with pork chops and salad.

Occasion _____ Date _____
Comments _____
_____

Princess Bread

5 cups Flour   1 tbsp. Butter, melted
2 tbsp. Baking Powder   2 cups Milk
1 tsp. Salt   Cooking Oil

Sift 4 cups flour with baking powder and salt. In a separate bowl, combine milk and melted butter. Place flour, baking powder in large bowl, add liquid ingredients, beating each in with a mixer. When the 4 cups are worked into a soft dough with milk, lightly flour the board with the remaining 1 cup flour. Turn the dough onto the board and knead lightly.

Divide the dough into 3 parts. Shape each into a round 1/8" thick that will fit your skillet. Heat oil and brown bread quickly one at a time until cooked. Serve cut into wedges with jam or stew.

Occasion _____ Date _____
Comments _____
_____

 Tip Removing chicken skin reduces fat 40 - 50%.

Winter Spoon Bread

1 cup sifted Cornmeal
1/4 cup Flour
3 tbsp. Sugar
1 tsp. Salt
4 cups Milk

½ cup Margarine
5 large Egg yolks
1 ½ tsp. Baking powder
1 cup Corn Kernels

Preheat oven to 375F. Grease a cast 12" iron skillet. Heat in oven.

Combine cornflour, sugar, salt and flour in a saucepan. Mix the milk and margarine and bring to a boil. Using a whisk, add dry ingredients to hot liquids in a stream. Put into bowl and cool.

In another bowl, beat 3 egg yolks with baking powder. Stir into cooled ingredients along with corn kernels.

In a clean bowl beat 5 egg whites to form stiff peaks. Gently fold into cooled ingredients. Carefully pour into hot skillet and return to oven for 25 minutes. Serve immediately with chicken or beef stew or hearty soup.

Occasion _____ Date _____

Comments _____
_____
_____
_____

Lighter Fare A lady was entertaining her friend's small son. "Are you sure you can cut your meat?" She asked, after watching his struggle. "Oh yes," he replied without looking up from his plate, "We often have it as tough as this at home."

Blue Corn Scones

½ cup blue Cornmeal
1 3/4 cup Flour
1/3 tsp. Baking powder
1/4 tsp. Salt
1/4 lb. Butter, chilled

1/4 cup Brown Sugar
1 Egg
½ cup Milk
½ tsp. Vanilla extract

Preheat oven to 375F. Grease and flour baking sheet.
Stir the dry ingredients in a bowl, then cut in butter to form a coarse meal.
Beat egg with milk, sugar and vanilla. When smooth, stir into the other mixture until the dough holds together. Knead briefly on a floured surface. Pat into an 8'" circle; place on baking sheet. Using pizza cutter, score circle into 8 wedges.   Bake for 15 - 20 minutes until nicely brown.
Serve with honey, fruits, jams or whipped cream. Best fresh from the oven, but can be served next day.

Occasion _____ Date _____
Comments _____

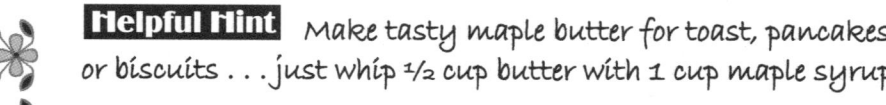

Buckskin Bread

2 cups Flour
1 tsp. Baking Powder

1 tsp. Salt
1 cup Water

Sift together dry ingredients, then quickly mix in water.
Press the dough into a 9" pie plate and bake at 400F. for 25 minutes. Cut into wedges and serve. Good for "sopping up" gravies.

Occasion _____ Date _____
Comments _____

Helpful Hint Make tasty maple butter for toast, pancakes or biscuits . . . just whip ½ cup butter with 1 cup maple syrup.

Wild Sage Bread

1 pkg. Dry Yeast	2 tsp. Sage
1 cup Cottage Cheese	½ tsp. Salt
1 Egg	1/4 tsp. Baking Soda
1 tbsp. Shortening, melted	2 ½ cups Flour
1 tbsp. Sugar	

Combine sugar, sage, salt, baking soda and flour. Dissolve yeast in 1/4 cup warm water. Beat egg and cottage cheese together until smooth. Add melted shortening and yeast.

Add flour mixture slowly to egg mixture, beating well after each addition, until a stiff dough is formed.

Cover dough with cloth and put in warm place until double in bulk (about 1 hour). Punch dough down, knead for one minute and place in well greased pan. Cover and let rise for 40 minutes.

Bake in a 350F. oven for 50 minutes. Brush top with melted shortening and sprinkle with crushed, roasted pine nuts or coarse salt.

Occasion _____ Date _____

Comments _____

_____

_____

_____

 Tip   When eating raw spinach, some of the vitamins and minerals pass unused through the body. Cooking solves this by helping to break down the vegetable's tough cellular walls to extract the nutrients. This allows the digestive system to better absorb them.

Indian Bean Bread

4 cups Cornmeal   2 cups cooked Kidney Beans
½ tsp. Baking Soda   2 cups boiling Water

Put cornmeal in bowl, mix in drained beans. Hollow out a hole and put in soda and water. Make dough stiff enough to form balls.

Drop balls into pot of boiling water. Cook 45 minutes. Serve sliced and fried in butter. Nice served with pork .

Occasion _____ Date _____
Comments _____

_____
_____
_____

Oneida Indian Fry Bread

8 cups Flour   2 tsp. Salt
Shortening   8 tsp. Baking Powder

Sift flour, baking powder and salt together, adding just enough water to make a dough. Knead about 3 minutes. Pinch off enough dough to make a round patty, flatten with hand and punch a hole in centre.

Drop in skillet of hot shortening and fry until light brown, turning once. Remove, drain on paper towels. Can be served with honey or jelly.

Occasion _____ Date _____
Comments _____

_____
_____

Lighter Fare The upper crust of society is just a bunch of rich crumbs held together by their own dough.

Herbed Bread Spread

½ cup Margarine
1 tsp. Parsley Flakes
1/4 tsp. Oregano

1 clove Garlic,
    minced
1/4 tsp. Dill Weed

Spread mixture onto a loaf of sliced Italian bread. Wrap in foil, except on top. Sprinkle with grated parmesan cheese and extra parsley.

Bake at 400F. for 10 minutes.

Occasion _____ Date _____

Comments _____

_____

_____

"Dande" Dipping Sauce

4 tbsp. Butter
2 medium Onions,
    chopped
3/4 lb. Fresh Dandelion
    Greens, chopped

4 cups Chicken Stock
1/4 lb. your favourite
    Sausage, chopped
1 loaf crusty Bread -
    French or Sourdough

Saute onions in butter until limp but not coloured.

Wash dandelion greens by submerging in water and drying on paper towels. Add dandelions to chicken stock, sausage and onions. Cover and simmer for 4 hours.

Serve with warm bread for dipping.   Serves 4 - 6.

Occasion _____ Date _____

Comments _____

_____

_____

Helpful Hint   Keep tiny pots of fresh growing herbs on the kitchen window sill . . . they'll be right at your fingertips for any recipe.

Roasted Garlic Spread

2 medium heads Garlic
2 X 8oz. pkg. Cream
   Cheese, softened
1 tsp. Thyme leaves

1 X 3 ½ oz. Goat
   Cheese
2 tbsp. Blue Cheese,
   crumbled

Preheat oven to 400F. Cut off tops of garlic and roast in pan for 45 minutes. Drizzle with olive oil. Remove and cool. Squeeze garlic out into bowl and mash.

Beat cream cheese and goat cheese in bowl until smooth. Stir in blue cheese, garlic and thyme. Refrigerate 3 hours. Spoon dip into serving bowl. Serve with veggies and garnish on plate with fresh thyme.

Occasion _____ Date _____

Comments _____

_____

Chicken Liver Pate

1/4 lb. Butter
1 Onion, minced
1 lb. Chicken Livers
4 tbsp. Brandy
1 tsp. Dry Mustard

1/4 tsp. Mace
1/4 tsp. Cloves
½ tsp. Green Pepper
Pinch of Cayenne
Salt to taste

Melt butter in skillet, add onions and saute until soft. Stir in livers and cook on medium heat until cooked. Puree mixture until smooth. Over medium heat pour brandy and scrape up the bits on bottom of pan. Add remaining ingredients blending until smooth. Pour in mould and chill. Serve with crackers or toast.

Occasion _____ Date _____

Comments _____

_____

 Tip A quick way to eliminate onion or garlic smell from your hands is to rinse in running water, rub them with baking soda, and rinse again.

Hot Onion & Chili Puffs

2 cups Flour
2 tbsp. Baking Powder
½ tsp. Salt
1 cup cold Milk
1/4 tsp. Thyme
1/4 tsp. Cumin
Oil for frying

1 Green Onion, all
  finely chopped
½ cup Cilantro, finely
  diced - or Parsley
1/4 tsp. Black Pepper
1/4 tsp. Chili Powder
2 tsp. Honey

In a large bowl, combine flour, baking powder and salt. Add onion, cilantro and spices. Make a well in the centre of flour, adding milk and honey. Stir dough well until all ingredients are blended. Dough will be sticky.

Heat one inch of oil in frying pan. Drop generously a tablespoon into hot oil. Fry to golden brown. Drain on towels.

Serve immediately. Makes 20. Prickly Pear Jelly is a good sauce to serve with these Puffs.

Occasion _____ Date _____

Comments _____
_____

Anchovy Spread

1/4 lb. Butter   1 tbsp. Anchovy spread

Blend in a food processor and use to spread on toasted melba rounds, vegetable rounds or pita triangles.

Occasion _____ Date _____

Comments _____
_____

Lighter Fare It does not require many words to speak the truth." - Chief Joseph

Pumpkin Molasses Tea Bread

2 cups all purpose Flour
½ tsp. Baking Powder
1 tsp. Baking Soda
1 tsp. Salt
½ cup Molasses
½ cup Sugar
½ cup Vegetable Oil
2 lg. Eggs, lightly beaten

1 cup cooked Pumpkin
2 tbsp. Apple Juice
½ cup dried Cranberries, roughly chopped
½ cup Walnuts, roughly chopped
8 oz. Cream Cheese, room temperature
1/4 cup Honey

Preheat oven to 350F. Butter and flour a 9 X 5" loaf pan. Set aside

Combine flour, baking powder, baking soda and salt in a medium bowl and set aside.

In bowl of electric mixer, beat molasses, sugar, oil, eggs, pumpkin and apple juice. Add flour mixture; mix until combined. Fold in cranberries and walnuts. Spoon mixture into prepared pan and bake about 1 hour.

Let the cake sit for about 10 minutes. Turn the read out of pan onto wire rack to cool completely.

While bread is cooling, make frosting. Combine cream cheese and honey in an electric mixing bowl and beat until smooth and well combined. Once bread is completely cooled, spread top with frosting. Serves 10.

Occasion _____ Date _____
Comments _____
_____
_____
_____

Tip   "we hold the Elders in great respect.
When they speak we listen, because they know more than us."
- Mary Muktoyuk

Acorn Bread

1 cup Acorn Meal
2 tbsp. Baking Powder
3 tbsp. Sugar
1 cup Milk

1 cup Flour
½ tsp. Salt
1 Egg, beaten
3 tbsp. Oil

Sift together acorn meal, white flour, baking powder, salt and sugar.   In a separate bowl, mix together egg, milk and oil.

Combine dry ingredients and liquid ingredients. Stir just enough to moisten dry ingredients.   Pour into a greased pan and bake at 400F. for 30 minutes.

Occasion _____ Date _____
Comments _____
_____
_____

Oatmeal Maple Bread

1 pkg. Yeast
1 cup Quick Oats
3 cups All Purpose Flour
1 tsp. Salt

1/3 cup Maple Syrup
1 tbsp. Oil
1 1/4 cups plus 1 tbsp.
   very warm water

Put all ingredients into the pan of your bread machine according to the instructions for your machine.   Use the white bread selection. Press start.

Makes 1 loaf.

Occasion _____ Date _____
Comments _____
_____
_____

Lighter Fare *Adam and Eve had the perfect marriage: he didn't have to hear about all the men she could have married; and she didn't have to hear about how well his mother cooked!*

Cranberry Bread

2 cups Flour	2 tbsp. Shortening,
½ tsp. Salt	melted
1 ½ tsp. Baking Soda	Boiling Water
1 cup Sugar	1 Egg, beaten
Juice and Zest from	1 cup Nuts, chopped
1 Orange	1 cup raw Cranberries

Put orange juice into a measuring cup. Add enough boiling water to make 1 cup. Add to dry ingredients, orange zest, orange juice and cranberries.

Add beaten egg. Mix well. Pour into 12oz. cans to bake (half full).

Bake for 1 hour 55 minutes at 325F.

Occasion _____ Date _____
Comments _____
_____
_____
_____

Helpful Hint Mahatma Gandhi was quite a spiritual person. He walked barefoot everywhere to the point that his feet became quite thick and hard. Even when he was not on a hunger strike, he didn't eat much. Over time he became quite thin and frail. Furthermore, due to his diet, he would end up with very bad breath. Therefore, he came to be known as a . . . "Super calloused fragile mystic plagued with halitosis."

Bacon Cornbread

1 1/3 cups Flour
1 cup Cornmeal
½ cup Sugar
1 ½ tsp. Baking Powder
½ tsp. Baking Soda
1 tsp. Salt
1 Egg, beaten

1 ½ cups Evaporated
   Milk
4 tsp. Vinegar
1/3 cup melted Butter
Bacon drippings
8 slices cooked Bacon,
   crumbled

Combine flour, cornmeal, sugar, baking powder, baking soda, salt and crumbled bacon.

In a separate bowl combine egg, milk and bacon drippings. Add flour and stir only until moistened.

Pour into greased 8" square pan. Bake at 350F. for 40 - 45 minutes. Serve warm with maple syrup.

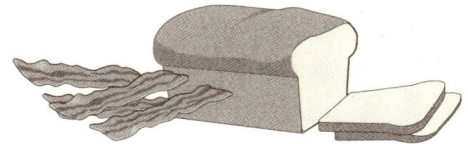

Occasion _____ Date _____
Comments _____
_____
_____
_____

Tip A funeral service was being held for a woman, and on carrying the casket out of the church, the pallbearers jarred it against the wall. A faint moan came forth. The woman was still alive. When she died a few years later, the husband warned the pallbearers, "Watch out for the wall!"

Breads and Spreads

Favourite Recipes from Family Members and Friends

(Recipes can be written in or pasted on)

B
R
E
A
D
S

&

S
P
R
E
A
D
S

Breads and Spreads

Favourite Recipes from Family Members and Friends

(Recipes can be written in or pasted on)

**B
R
E
A
D
S
&
S
P
R
E
A
D
S**

Delectable Desserts

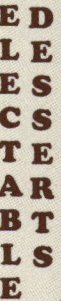

Baked Indian Pudding

½ cup Cornmeal
4 cups hot,
   homogenized Milk
½ cup Maple Syrup
1/4 cup Molasses
2 Eggs, slightly beaten

2 tbsp. Butter, melted
1/3 Brown Sugar, packed
1 tsp. Salt
1/4 tsp. Cinnamon
3/4 tsp. Ginger
½ cup Milk

In top of double boiler, slowly stir cornmeal into hot milk. Cook over boiling water, stirring occasionally for 20 minutes.

Preheat oven to 300F. Lightly grease a 2 quart baking dish.

In small bowl, combine remaining ingredients, except milk. Stir into cornmeal mixture. Mix well. Turn into prepared dish. Pour milk on top, without stirring.

Bake, uncovered for 2 hours or just until set , but quivery on top. Do not overbake. Let stand 30 minutes before serving.

Occasion _____ Date _____
Comments _____
_____
_____
_____

Lighter Fare   The recipe is certainly silly. It says to separate two eggs, but it doesn't say how far to separate them.   - Gracie Allen

Indian Rice Pudding

2 1/3 cup raw long grain white Rice
Water
1 tsp. Salt
1/4 tsp. powdered Saffron
2 cups Sugar
1 ½ cups Butter
2 whole Cardamon Seeds, shelled
5 whole Cloves
Juice of 1 Lemon
1/4 cup light Raisins
1/4 cup dark Raisins
1/4 cup unroasted Pistachios
1/4 cup blanched Almonds, sliced and toasted
1/4 cup unsalted Cashews
Brazil nuts, sliced and toasted
1 cup heavy Cream, whipped

Cook rice in 6 cups boiling water. Add salt and saffron. Cook about 10 minutes. Use enough saffron to give rich yellow colour. Drain. Boil sugar and 3 3/4 cup water until sugar dissolved.

In the bottom of a heavy Dutch oven, heat the butter. Add the cardamon and cloves and cook over low heat for 10 minutes. Add about ½ cup Syrup and boil one minute. Add rice and cook stirring gently until water is absorbed, about 10 minutes.

Add lemon juice, raisins, nuts. Cook on high about 5 minutes. Cover over low heat until rice is tender. If rice is not tender enough, add remaining syrup and cook until rice is dry and soft. Remove from heat, let stand covered about 10 minutes. Serve warm with whipped cream. Serves 12.

Occasion _____ Date _____
Comments _____
_____
_____
_____

Helpful Hint Named placecards for the table couldn't be easier to display. Tuck them into sections of a pine cone!

Quick Maple Upside Down Pudding

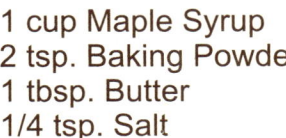

1 cup Maple Syrup	3 tbsp. Brown Sugar
2 tsp. Baking Powder	1 cup sifted Flour
1 tbsp. Butter	1 Egg
1/4 tsp. Salt	½ cup Milk

Heat maple syrup to boiling and pour into bottom of buttered baking dish. Cream shortening, add sugar and cream together until fluffy.

Sift flour, baking powder, salt and add alternately with milk in small amounts, beating well. Pour batter into hot syrup and bake in hot (425F.) oven for 25 minutes.

Turn upside down onto serving plate and garnish with chopped nuts and whipped cream. Or serve like a pudding in bowls with nuts and plain cream poured over.

Occasion _____ Date _____

Comments _____

_____

_____

Sour Cream Raisin Pie

1 cup Sugar	1/4 tsp. Cinnamon
1/4 tsp. Nutmeg	1 cup chick Sour Cream
3 Eggs, slightly beaten	2 cups Raisins
1 tsp. Salt	1 uncooked Pie Shell

Combine all ingredients and turn into pie shell. Bake in hot oven at 450F. for 15 minutes. Then reduce heat to 350F. for 30 minutes.

Occasion _____ Date _____

Comments _____

_____

_____

Lighter Fare *A delicious yummy serving of French Vanilla Ice cream adds 18g of fat, the equivalent of eating 450 rice cakes.*

Custard Bread Pudding

In a bowl, combine 4 eggs, 4 cups milk, ½ cup cream and 1 cup sugar until well blended.

Add 2 cups stale bread or toast buttered to egg mixture until moist. Add ½ tsp. Vanilla and mix. Then top with a light sprinkling of nutmeg.

Cook in 350F. oven in a water bath until knife comes out clean. About 1 hour.

Serve warm with whipped cream. For variation, add 1/4 cup each of chopped pecans, raisins or dried apricots

Sauce:

2 cups powdered Sugar	1/4 tsp. Rum extract
2 tbsp. Milk	½ cup cooled browned Butter

Heat butter in pan until it turns brown. Do not burn. Serve over warm bread pudding.

Occasion _____ Date _____

Comments _____

Wild Raspberry Bread Pudding

10 cups wild Raspberries, cleaned, dried	12 sliced White Bread, homemade
2 cups sugar	2 cups heavy Cream

In a large bowl, sprinkle sugar over raspberries. Toss berries lightly, cover and set aside.

Cut slice of bread to fit in bottom of deep 2 quart bowl. Trim 8 or 9 slices of bread into wedges about 4 inches at the top and 3 inches across the bottom. Line sides of bowl with wedges, overlapping each one by about ½ inch.

Pour fruit into bowl and cover top completely with rest of bread. Cover top of bowl with a flat plate and place a weight on top of plate. Refrigerate 12 hours. Remove from mould inverting on a plate. Decorate with whipped cream, covering mould completely. Serve chilled.

Occasion _____ Date _____

Comments _____

Lighter Fare I told my doctor I get very tired when I go on a diet, so he gave me pep pills. Know what happened? I ate faster! - Joe E. Lewis

Rhubarb Custard Pie

3 cups diced Rhubarb   1 ½ cups Sugar or Equal
1/4 tsp. Salt   3 tbsp. Flour
1 tbsp. Lemon Juice   1 X 9" Pie shell
2 Eggs, separated

Cut rhubarb into small pieces and arrange in an unbaked pie shell. Mix together remaining ingredients including egg yolks and pour this mixture over rhubarb. Cover with meringue made from the egg whites.

Bake in hot oven for 425F. for 10 minutes then reduce heat to 350F. and bake 30 minutes.

Occasion _____ Date _____

Comments _____

_____

_____

Black Walnut Souffle

1 cup Walnuts   ½ cup Sugar
½ cup Cream   6 Eggs, separated
1/4 lb. Butter

In a bowl, cream butter. Add egg yolks, one at a time beating between each addition.   Then add cream, sugar and nuts, beating continuously.

Whip egg whites until stiff and fold into creamy mixture.   Pour into a greased souffle dish and bake at 375F. for 1 hour.

Occasion _____ Date _____

Comments _____

_____

_____

Helpful Hint Running ice cold water over the kernels of popcorn before popping will help to eliminate uncooked kernels.

Diabetic Dutch Apple Pie

1/4 cup Flour
½ quick Oats
½ tsp. Cinnamon
5 cups sliced Apples

½ cup unsweetened frozen
  Apple Juice concentrate
Sweetener equal to ½ cup
  sugar
Pie crust

Mix flour, oats, cinnamon and sweetener with a fork. Pour over sliced apples and mix well. Pour apple juice over top of apples and mix well again. Put apple mixture in pie crust. Set aside.

Topping:
1/4 cup Flour
½ cup Quick Oats
Sweetener = to ½
  cup brown sugar

1 tsp. Cinnamon
1 pkg. Sugarfree Instant
  Vanilla Pudding mix
½ cup Margarine

Mix dry ingredients with fork. Add butter and cut into dry ingredients with a pastry blender or 2 knives until it resembles coarse crumbs. Pour mixture over pie filling and press down evenly over apples.

Bake at 400F. for 45 - 55 minutes.

251 calories.

Occasion _____ Date _____
Comments _____
_____
_____

 Tip To clean coffee grinder, grind ½ cup
uncooked rice through your coffee grinder.

Diabetic Rhubarb and Apple Crumble

2 ½ cups chopped
   fresh Rhubarb
3 Granny Smith Apples,
   peeled and diced
2 tbsp. Cornstarch
2 ½ tsp. Equal Sweetener

1/3 cup Water or
   Apple Juice
1 tbsp. Lemon Juice
2 tsp. finely grated
   Lemon Peel

Toss together rhubarb, apples, cornstarch and Equal. Place in 1 ½ quart casserole dish.

Combine water, lemon juice and lemon peel pouring mixture over fruit. Cover and bake in preheated 400F. oven until rhubarb is tender ~ about 15 minutes. Spoon topping evenly over fruit and bake until crisp.

Serve warm with frozen yoghurt or ice cream.

Topping:
½ cup Minute Oats
1/4 cup Bran Cereal
1/4 cup Raisins

1/4 cup Walnuts
2 ½ tsp. Equal
1 tbsp. Butter

Blend together.

Occasion _____ Date _____
Comments _____
_____
_____

Cranberry Fritters

2 cups Cranberries,
   washed & diced
3/4 cup Flour
2 Eggs, well beaten
3/4 tsp. Salt

1/4 tsp. Pepper
1 tsp. Butter, melted
1 tbsp. Brandy Extract
Powdered Sugar

Combine eggs, flour, salt, pepper and brandy together. Mix well.

Drop by tablespoonful in hot fat at 350F. until crisp and brown. Drain on paper towels.

Sift powdered sugar on them. Serve warm.

Occasion _____ Date _____

Comments _____

_____

_____

Hickory Nut Cake

½ cup Butter
1 tsp. Baking Soda
1 cup Hickory Nuts
1 cup Sugar
2 Eggs

1 tsp. Cream of Tartar
1 cup Sour Cream or
   Milk
Salt
1 3/4 cup Flour

Mix all ingredients together. Bake in 350F. oven until done.

Occasion _____ Date _____

Comments _____

_____

_____

Helpful Hint Brown sugar won't harden if an apple slice is placed in the container.

Butternut Cake

1 ½ cups Sugar	3 Eggs
2 cups Flour	½ cup Milk
1 tsp. Baking Soda	2 tsp. Cream of Tartar
½ cup Butter, melted	

Combine flour, soda, cream of tartar and sugar. Mix in butter, eggs and milk.   Grease pans and pour the batter in.

Bake at 350F. for 35 - 45 minutes in two 8" round pans.

Filling:

2 cups Butternuts, pulverized	1 tbsp. Sugar
1 cup sweet Cream	1 tsp. Cornstarch, mixed with 2 tbsp. cold Milk

To Make Filling:

Let cream come to a boil, then stir in cornstarch and sugar. Bring to a boil again, and remove from stove. Stir in butternuts. When partially cooled, spread between the two layers.

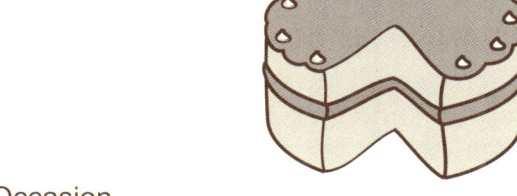

Occasion _____ Date _____

Comments _____

_____

_____

 Tip   To deal with fruit flies, place a dish of apple cider vinegar out. Flies will head straight for the vinegar and drown.

14 Minute Maple Fudge

1 cups Maple Syrup
1 cup Whipping Cream

1/4 cup Butter
1 cup chopped Nuts
1 tsp. Lemon Extract

Starting cold, cook maple syrup, cream and butter together at a gentle boil for 9 minutes after boiling point is reached. Remove from heat, add nuts and lemon, stirring vigorously with wooden spoon for 5 minutes.

Pour into buttered pans. Cool. Cut into squares.

Occasion _____ Date _____

Comments _____

_____

Pear & Ginger Upside Down Cake

2 unpeeled Pears, cored
   and sliced
3 tbsp. fresh Lemon Juice
1 - 2 tbsp. Melted Butter
1/3 cup Skim Milk
3 tbsp. Apricot Spread,
   unsweetened
1 tbsp. Vegetable Oil

1 tbsp. fresh Ginger,
   minced
1 - 2 tbsp. packed
   Brown Sugar
1 cup Flour
1 tsp. Baking Powder
1/4 tsp. Baking Soda
1 tsp. Cinnamon
1/8 tsp. Salt

Preheat oven to 375F. Spray 10" deep dish with cooking spray. Toss pears in lemon juice. Drain. Brush butter onto bottom of prepared pan. Sprinkle sugar over butter. Arrange pears in dish. Bake 10 minutes.

In the meantime, combine flour, baking powders, baking soda, cinnamon and salt in small bowl. Set aside. Combine milk, apricot spread, egg, oil and ginger in medium bowl. Mix well. Add flour mixture and stir well. Carefully spread batter evenly over pears and to edges of pan.

Bake 20 to 25 minutes. Cool 5 minutes. Place plate over pan and invert. Use knife to loosen cake. Serve warm.

Occasion _____ Date _____

Comments _____

_____

Lighter Fare   Old people shouldn't eat health foods. They need all the preservatives they can get!

Cranberry Nut Squares

1 cup Flour   ½ cup light Brown Sugar
½ cup soft Butter

Bottom:
   In a food processor, combine flour and brown sugar. Add butter, pulse until dough clumps together. Pat dough into a greased 11 X 7" baking pan.

   Bake at 350F. for 15 minutes or until golden around edges. Remove from oven and cool.

Topping:
1 cup Brown Sugar   2 large Eggs
½ cup dark Corn Syrup   1 cup Walnuts, coarsely
2 tsp. Vanilla   chopped
2 tbsp. Butter   3/4 cup dried Cranberries
2 tbsp. Flour   ½ cup Coconut, large
                             flakes

   Cook together topping ingredients for 10 minutes until sugars are dissolved. Spread over bottom crust. Bake 25 - 30 minutes or until golden brown. Cool and cut into squares.

   Makes approximately 24.

Occasion _____ Date _____
Comments _____
_____
_____
_____

Helpful Hint   To speed up the process of turning green tomatoes red, put items in a brown paper bag with an apple.

Delectable Desserts

Favourite Recipes from Family Members and Friends
(Recipes can be written in or pasted on)

Delectable Desserts

Favourite Recipes from Family Members and Friends
(Recipes can be written in or pasted on)

D
E
L
E
C
T
A
B
L
E

D
E
S
S
E
R
T
S

Fish and Game

Baked Pickerel

2 large Pickerel Fillets
½ small Onion, chopped
2 oz. Butter

1 Lemon, sliced
1 - 2 Bay leaves
Salt & Pepper

Preheat oven to 350F.

Place fillets on parchment paper. Between them, place salt and pepper, lemon, onion, bay leaf and butter. Roll up and prick with fork. Bake approximately 20 minutes. Serves 6.

Fried Pickerel with a Crispy Crumb Coating

1 pkg. Salted Crackers
½ tsp. Garlic Salt

1/4 cup Flour
1/4 tsp. fresh Green Pepper

Combine above ingredients and set aside.

In a bowl, beat 1 egg and 1 cup milk.

Cut fish in small pieces and dip in egg wash. Roll fish in crumbs. Fry in skillet on high heat for 3 - 4 minutes. Drain on paper towels. Serve right away.

Occasion _____ Date _____
Comments _____
_____

Tip If a person has a fishbone stuck in their throat, often a small chunk of bread will usually force the bone down to avoid choking.

Roast Loin of Venison
with Cranberries

2 thick slices of Lemon	2 thick slices of Orange
1 cup Sugar	2 slices peeled fresh Ginger
2 cups frozen Cranberries	2 small Bay leaf

Prepare 1 day ahead.

In a medium non-reactive saucepan, combine lemon, orange, ginger, sugar and bay leaf with 1 cup of cranberry juice. Bring to boil over high heat, stirring to dissolve sugar. Reduce heat to moderate and boil, uncovered until syrupy ~ 10 to 15 minutes.

Stir in the cranberries, then remove from heat and cool. Transfer the mixture to a glass container, cover and refrigerate for 1 to 2 days, stirring once or twice during that time.

4 lbs. boneless Loin of Venison, room temperature	2 cups Cranberry Juice
	2 tbsp. cold Butter, cut in pieces
1 tsp. Salt	2 cups Beef Stock
1 1/4 tsp. Pepper	Fresh Thyme sprigs, for garnish
3/4 tsp. finely chopped Juniper Berries	

Preheat oven to 400F. Rub the venison with the olive oil, 3/4 tsp. salt, 1 tsp. pepper and ½ tsp. chopped juniper berries, pressing the seasonings in to the meat. Set the loin on a rack in a roasting pan and roast, basting frequently with the pan juices, until medium-rare (about 135F. on a meat thermometer) for 45 minutes. Cover the venison loosely with foil and set aside for 10 to 15 minutes before carving.

Meanwhile, remove and discard bay leaf, lemon, orange and ginger slices from the cranberries. In a food processor or blender, puree half the cranberries and half the liquid until smooth.

In a medium non-reactive saucepan, boil wine over high heat until reduced to ½ cup, about 5 minutes. Add the stock and remaining cranberry juice and bring to boil. Add cranberry puree, reduce the heat to low and simmer, uncovered until slightly thickened, about 10 minutes. Remove from heat.

Strain remaining whole cranberries and add them to the sauce with the remaining 1/4 tsp. Salt, pepper and chopped juniper berries. Swirl in the cold butter.

Slice the venison thinly. Stir any juices into the sauce, and serve with the sauce reheated if necessary. Garnish with fresh thyme sprigs.

Occasion _____ Date _____

Comments _____

_____

Iroquois Venison Roast

4 - 6 lbs. Boneless Roast	1 bottle Apple Cider
1 cup Flour	Vinegar
1 medium Onion, chopped	Salt and pepper
in pieces	1/8 cup ground Cloves
2 Bay leaves	1/8 cup Allspice

Slit sides and top at 3" intervals and stuff in pieces of onion.

Mix together bay leaf, cloves, salt, pepper, allspice and oil. Rub into and all over roast.   Cover meat with vinegar in a covered dish for 12 hours in refrigerator.

To cook, lift out meat, roll in flour and braise all sides quickly in 1/8 cup hot oil.   Pour on vinegar marinade and cook 20 minutes per pound at 350F.   Let sit for 20 minutes after removing from oven. Slice. Serve drippings on the side.

Occasion _____ Date _____

Comments _____
_____
_____
_____

Lighter Fare When the waitress brought him the soup du jour, the Englishman was a bit dismayed. 'Good heavens, what's this?' he said. "Why, it's bean soup," she replied. "I don't care what it has been," he sputtered, "What is it now?"

Wild Goose with
Apples & Raisin Stuffing

1 X 8-10 lb. Wild Goose, dressed	1 lg. cooking Apple, chopped
½ cup Lemon Juice	½ cup Raisins
1 tsp. Salt	4 cups Breadcrumbs
½ tsp. Pepper	½ tsp. Salt
½ cup Margarine	1/4 tsp. Pepper
1 Onion, chopped	6 slices Bacon
½ cup Celery	1/4 cup Bacon Fat
	1/4 cup fresh Rosemary

Place goose in a roasting pan. Sprinkle inside and out with lemon juice, salt and pepper.

Melt margarine in skillet, add onions, celery and rosemary. Saute until translucent. Add apples, raisins, breadcrumbs, salt and pepper.   Set aside to cool.   Pack stuffing lightly into cavity. Close opening.

Rub goose with bacon fat. Place strips of bacon over goose. Cover and roast at 350F. for 30 minutes per pound. Baste frequently.

Occasion _____ Date _____
Comments _____
_____
_____
_____

 Tip To help peel most fruit more easily, blanch them for 45 seconds in boiling water.

Roast Quail

1 Quail, quartered
1/4 cup Butter
½ cup diced Onion
2 tbsp. fresh, chopped
   Parsley

2 tbsp. Maple Syrup
½ cup Celery
1 tbsp. Cornstarch
1 cup Chicken Stock
1 cup sliced Mushrooms

Dry quail and saute in butter for 10 minutes. Remove quail and saute onion and celery in butter remaining in the pan for about 5 minutes.

Reduce heat. Add cornstarch dissolved in stock and cook, stirring constantly until thickened. Stir in maple syrup. Arrange quail in shallow casserole dish and pour sauce over them.

While quail is baking, saute mushrooms in 1 tbsp. oil. Sprinkle over fowl with parsley when serving on platter.

Occasion _____ Date _____

Comments _____

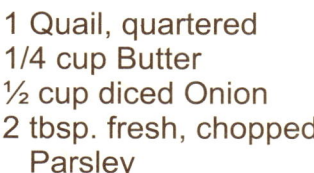

Roast Wild Pheasant

½ cup Grape Jelly
½ cup Water
1 Pheasant, dressed
Lemon Juice

1 cup Celery
1 cup Onion, chopped
Salt and Pepper
1 cup Margarine

Wash and pat meat dry. Wipe cavity well with lemon juice. Combine celery and onion, cook briefly. Stuff cavity but do not close. Fold wings over back and truss.

Place breast side up on a rack in roasting pan. Add ½ cup water, cover and roast 350F. Allow 15 - 20 minutes per pound.

When meat is cooked, add grape jelly to drippings. Cook uncovered for 15 minutes, basting frequently.

Occasion _____ Date _____

Comments _____

Helpful Hint For the flakiest pie crust, brush lightly with cold water just before putting in oven.

Hush Puppies with Fried Fish

2 ½ cups self rising Cornmeal   1 Egg, well beaten
3 tbsp. self rising Flour   1 cup Milk
4 tsp. finely chopped Onion   Your favourite Fish, cut up

    Combine cornmeal, flour and chopped onion.   Add egg and gradually stir in the milk.
    Drop the batter by tablespoonful into the hot fat ~ 375F. Save aside some batter to coat fish.
    Cook hush puppies first and then cook fish.

Occasion _____ Date _____
Comments _____
_____

Poached Salmon

6 X 1" Salmon Steaks   2 tsp. Parsley
6 - 8 Mushrooms, sliced   2 Green Onions, all chopped
1 red Pepper, finely   1 qt. Water or Chicken stock
   chopped   Black Pepper
Salt & Pepper to taste   Lemon wedges

    Combine mushrooms, parsley, scallions, bell pepper, salt and pepper in chicken broth.   Bring to a boil, reduce heat and simmer 8 minutes.   Cook broth to room temperature.
    Place steaks in saucepan. Cover with broth. Simmer 15 - 20 minutes.   Serve each with broth and lemon wedges. Serves 6.

Occasion _____ Date _____
Comments _____
_____

Lighter Fare   "I've been on a constant diet for the last 2 decades. I've lost a total of 789 pounds. By all accounts, I should be hanging from a charm bracelet. - Erma Bombeck

Fried Rabbit

1 Rabbit, skinned
   and cut up
1 cup Flour
1 tsp. Salt

1 Onion, diced
1/4 Lemon, juiced
Cooking Oil
Pepper to taste

Roll rabbit pieces in a mix of flour, salt and pepper. Brown in 4 tbsp. of oil.   After all are browned, add onion and lemon juice.

Cover and cook until done.

Occasion _____ Date _____

Comments _____

Coureur de Bois Casserole

Wild Game - approx. 1 1/2 - 2 lbs. Caribou, Moose, Deer
   or Rabbit   2 medium Onions, chopped
1/4 cup Olive Oil   2 cups cold Beef Boullion

Preheat oven to 3250F.   On stove heat oil and saute onion until slightly browned.   Braise meat.

Place meat in ovenproof casserole dish and add cold boullion.   At 3250F. cook 30 minutes then turn down oven to 2500F. for 3 - 6 hours depending on meat chosen.

Half an hour before end of cooking time, add sliced potatoes and carrots to broth and meat. Serve with hot rolls or hearty grain bread.

Occasion _____ Date _____

Comments _____

Tip To remove rust from your cutlery, rub with cut onion. Leave onion juice on for one hour or more, then rinse and dry well.

Fish and Game

Favourite Recipes from Family Members and Friends
(Recipes can be written in or pasted on)

F
I
S
H

&

G
A
M
E

Fish and Game

Favourite Recipes from Family Members and Friends
(Recipes can be written in or pasted on)

F
I
S
H

&

G
A
M
E

Kreations for Kids

61

Blanket Dog

3 cups Flour   1 ½ tsp. Salt
1 tbsp. Baking Powder   1 ½ cups Water
                  12 Wieners

Mix all ingredients gently. Separate 2 tbsp. and pat out with roll out into rectangular shape. Place wiener on bannock and roll up until wiener is covered with dough.

Fry in vegetable oil until brown. Remove and drain on paper towels. Serve with melted cheese, ketchup or mustard. Serves 12.

Occasion _____ Date _____
Comments _____
_____
_____
_____

Strawberry Banana Sherbert

1 qt. Strawberries,   ½ cup Sugar
   washed and chopped   1 cup Orange Juice
4 Bananas, mashed   2 cups Milk
Ice Cube trays

Mix all ingredients and pour into ice cube trays and place in freezer until frozen. Take out and put into tall milkshake glasses (6 each).

Occasion _____ Date _____
Comments _____
_____
_____
_____

Helpful Hint Dissolve a teaspoon of gelatin into whipped cream before beating, and it will hold for an hour more.

Mohawk Taco Pizza

1 ½ lb. Ground beef
1 ½ tsp. Taco Seasoning
1/4 cup Chunky Salsa
1 pkg. of 12 medium flour Tortillas
1 ½ cups shredded 3-Cheese
  blend

Pizza Toppings:
Sliced Mushrooms
Green Peppers
Sliced Olives
Green Onions
Chopped Tomatoes

In a large skillet, brown ground beef. Drain. Stir in seasoning, add salsa and cook thoroughly.

Place tortillas on baking sheet. Divide beef mixture spreading to edges. Top pizzas with desired toppings. Sprinkle with cheese.

Bake at 400F. for 8 to 10 minutes. Makes 12 pizzas.

Occasion _____ Date _____
Comments _____
_____

Fruit Smoothie

1 cup Orange Juice
1 cup plain Yoghurt
1 Banana, chunked

1 cup frozen Strawberries
  or Raspberries, unsweetened
1/4 cup Equal

Place all ingredients in blender or food processor and blend until smooth. Serves 3. Top with whipped cream and/or fresh strawberry.

Occasion _____ Date _____
Comments _____
_____

 Tip Did you know you would have to eat 200 pretzels to consume the same amount of calories in one hotdog?

Vanilla Sugar Cookie Snowmen

3/4 cup Sugar
6 tbsp. Unsalted Butter
1/3 cup Shortening
1 large Egg
1 tbsp. Milk

1 tsp. Vanilla
2 cups Flour
1 ½ tsp. Baking
   Powder
1/4 tsp. Salt

In a large bowl using an electric mixer, cream sugar, butter and shortening until fluffy. Add egg, milk and vanilla, beating well.

In a small bowl, combine flour, baking powder and salt. Add to butter mixture, mixing on medium until combined well.

Turn dough onto a large piece of plastic wrap, seal up and refrigerate at least 2 hours.

Work with half the dough at a time. Relax dough by letting it sit 30 minutes. Cut into desired shapes and cook at 375F. for 8 - 10 minutes. Cool on rack and decorate.   Have fun creating each individual cookie!

Occasion _____ Date _____
Comments _____
_____
_____
_____

Lighter Fare How do you catch a "unique rabbit?" U - nique up on it! How do you catch a "tame rabbit?" The tame way! You nique up on it!"

Grandma Green's Award Winning
Peanut Butter Cookies

1 cup Peanut Butter   1 cup Brown Sugar   1 Egg

Mix ingredients together. Make 2" balls and flatten with a fork.

Bake at 350F. for 8 - 10 minutes or until done. They may seem soft and not cooked, but they are! And they will harden, tasting deliciously peanut buttery!

Recently won by my Grandson, Dakota.

Occasion _____ Date _____
Comments _____
_____

Fudge

1 cup Sugar
½ tsp. Salt
3 tbsp. Unsalted Butter
½ cup heavy Cream

1 3/4 cup mini Marshmallows
1 ½ cups Chocolate Chips
½ tsp. Vanilla
Optional: chopped Peppermints

Line a 9" X 5" loaf pan with wax paper.

Combine sugar, salt, butter, cream and marshmallows in a heavy bottomed saucepan. Melt butter and marshmallows. Bring to a boil for 5 minutes, stirring occasionally. Add chocolate chips and vanilla, stirring until melted. Add peppermint pieces and/or nuts, if desired.

Pour into pan and top with nuts. Cool at room temperature for 3 hours. Cut into squares. Makes 24.

Occasion _____ Date _____
Comments _____

Helpful Hint Put soft chocolate chip cookies in a newly emptied coffee can, seal and freeze. When thawed, the cookies will have a tasty mocha flavour.

Gingerbread Kids

1 cup unsalted Butter
1 cup firmly packed
  Dark Brown Sugar
1 large Egg
½ cup unsulphured
  Molasses

2 1/4 tsp. Cinnamon
2 tsp. Ginger
1 tsp. Allspice
1 tsp. Baking soda
1/4 tsp. Salt
4 cups Flour

In a large bowl beat butter and sugar on high speed until light and fluffy ~ about 5 minutes. Add egg and mix well. Beat in molasses, cinnamon, ginger, allspice, baking soda and salt. On low speed, add flour a cup at a time mixing until incorporated.

Divide dough into quarters, shape into rounds and wrap in plastic. Refrigerate until firm ~ about 3 hours.

Preheat oven to 375F. Roll and cut out cookies. Dress and decorate each one as a kid ~ boy and girl, with hair, clothes and jewellery from icing and scraps.

Occasion _____ Date _____

Comments _____

_____

_____

_____

⚠ Tip   Licking a postage stamp will set you back anywhere from 2 to 8 calories, depending on how vigorously you lick it!

Favourite Birthday Cake

3/4 cup Shortening
1 ½ tsp. Vanilla
3 tsp. Baking Powder
1 cup Milk
1 ½ cups Sugar

2 1/4 cups sifted
   Cake Flour
1 tsp. Salt
5 stiffly beaten Egg
   Whites

Cream shortening and sugar until light and fluffy. Add vanilla and mix well.

Sift together flour, baking powder and salt. Add to creamed mixture alternately with milk, beating after each addition.

Gently fold in egg whites. Bake in 2 greased and lightly floured pans of your choice. Any shape is fine.

Bake at 375F. for 18 - 20 minutes.

Growing up, my mother would wrap a nickel in wax paper and cook it in the cake. We always were surprised to see who got it in their slice!

Occasion _____ Date _____

Comments _____

_____

_____

_____

Lighter Fare   Little Johnny swallowed a quarter.
He started to choke. Someone yelled, "Get
the pastor; he knows how to get money out of people."

Toffee

1 cup chopped Nuts	½ cup Butter
½ cup semi-sweet	3/4 cup Brown Sugar,
Chocolate Chips	packed

Butter an 8"X8" pan, and spread walnuts on bottom.
In a saucepan, heat butter and sugar, bringing to boil and stirring constantly. Cook until mixture darkens ~ about 7 minutes. Pour over walnuts. Sprinkle chocolate chips over top. Cover baking sheet to hold in heat to melt chocolate. Spread chips over top.

Cut into 1 ½ " squares. Refrigerate. Break into squares when cool. Makes about one pound.

Occasion _____ Date _____
Comments _____
_____
_____

Molasses Popcorn Balls

4 qts. popped Popcorn	4 tbsp. Sugar
1 cup Molasses	1 tsp. Baking Powder
	1 tsp. Butter

Place popcorn in a large bowl. Set aside.
Bring molasses and sugar to a boil in a large pan. Boil for 20 minutes to soft ball stage. Remove from heat, stirring in quickly the baking soda and butter. Pour mixture over popcorn.

Grease hands with butter and shape popcorn into apple size balls. Wrap in plastic.

Occasion _____ Date _____
Comments _____
_____
_____

Helpful Hint Submerging a lemon in hot water for 15 minutes before squeezing will make it yield almost twice as much juice.

Ice Cream Brownie Bars

Melt a 6 oz. Valrona chocolate bar in a double boiler with 1 ½ sticks (12 tbsp.) unsalted creamy butter.

Whisk together 3 large eggs in a bowl with a pinch of salt, 1 cup sugar, ½ cup light brown sugar and 1 tsp. Vanilla. Pour chocolate into mixture. Sift 3/4 cup flour and mix in together.

Pour into a 9"X 13" lined pan. Cook at 325F. for 20 minutes. Cool brownie, put on larger piece of parchment or waxed paper and return to pan and freeze.

Put 2 pints ice cream on top of brownie and freeze. Add 2 more pints and freeze more. Keep returning bars to freezer to keep from melting between stages.

Melt 40 oz. Chocolate in double boiler.

Cut brownie into 12 bars and refreeze. Put out individually on a tray and ladle chocolate over bars, completely covering the bars. Return to freezer.

Serve individually on plate.

Occasion _____ Date _____

Comments _____

_____

_____

_____

 Tip Share silly memories at your next family get-to-gether. Ask everyone to jot down their favourites and toss in a hat, pulling them out one by one and reading out loud. Guaranteed giggles!

Pumpkin Waffles

2 1/4 cups Flour
1/4 cup Brown Sugar, packed
4 tsp. Baking Powder
1 ½ tsp. Cinnamon
½ cup Pecans

1 tsp. Nutmeg
1/4 tsp. Cloves
½ tsp. Ginger
4 Eggs, separated
1 cup canned Pumpkin
1/4 cup Butter, melted

Combine first 7 ingredients and set aside.

In separate bowl, mix together egg yolks, milk and pumpkin. Add to flour mixture, stirring until just moistened. Stir in butter and set aside.

Beat egg whites at high speed until soft peaks form. Fold into waffle batter.

Heat oiled waffle iron according to manufacturer's directions. Pour batter into hot iron. Bake 4 - 5 minutes. Makes 12 - 16 waffles.

Serve with butter, maple syrup sprinkled with toasted. pecans.

Occasion _____ Date _____
Comments _____
_____
_____
_____

 Why do gorillas have big nostrils?
Because they have big fingers!

Zippy Oven Fries

1 lb. Potatoes, sliced into 1/4" wedges
3 tbsp. Butter or Oil
2 tbsp. Cayenne Pepper sauce
2 cups French Fried Onions in can, finely chopped
½ cup Parmesan Cheese

Preheat oven to 400F. Place potatoes, butter and hot sauce in a plastic bag and shake up.

Add potatoes to already spread out french fried onions and cheese, coating completely.

Arrange on a greased shallow baking pan. Bake uncovered 25 minutes or until done. Serves 4 - 6.

Occasion _____ Date _____
Comments _____

Fish Nuggets

2 lbs. Pickerel Fillets
½ large Onion, minced
½ cup Cornmeal
½ cup Flour
½ cup Milk

1 Egg
Salt & Pepper to taste
Dash of Garlic Powder
Oil for frying

Cut pickerel in nugget sizes. Dredge in egg and milk mixture, then roll in cornmeal and flour mix including salt and pepper, garlic and onion.

Fry in oil and drain on paper towels. Serve with Zippy Oven Fries for classic fish and chips.

Occasion _____ Date _____
Comments _____
_____

Helpful Hint Ask for butter, gravy, sauces and salad dressings on the side. This allows you to limit your fat intake.

Blueberry Dumplings

3 pints Blueberries   1 cup Sugar
3/4 cup Water   1 ½ tbsp. Butter

Combine in a pan and let sit while preparing second part.

2 cups Flour   1 Egg
3 tbsp. Sugar   3 ½ tsp. Baking Powder
1 tsp. Salt   Milk

Sift flour, sugar, salt and baking powder in bowl. Add eggs and mix well. Add enough milk to make stiff batter.

Bring part one to a boil. Drop dumpling batter in, a spoonful at a time into boiling mixture. Cover with lid and cook for about 15 - 20 minutes.

Serve with whipped cream or ice cream.

Occasion _____ Date _____

Comments _____
_____
_____
_____

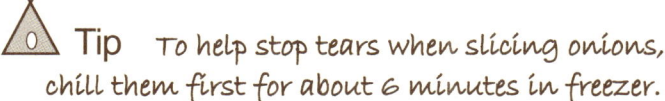

Tip   To help stop tears when slicing onions, chill them first for about 6 minutes in freezer.

Kreations for Kids

Favourite Recipes from Family Members and Friends
(Recipes can be written in or pasted on)

K
R
E
A
T
I
O
N
S

for

K
I
D
S

Kreations for Kids

Favourite Recipes from Family Members and Friends
(Recipes can be written in or pasted on)

K
R
E
A
T
I
O
N
S
f
o
r
K
I
D
S

Marvellous Meat Dishes

Chicken & Nut Stir Fry

1 lb. Pork or boneless
  Chicken Breasts
1/4 cup Honey
½ cup Terriyaki Sauce
1/4 cup Orange Juice

2 tbsp. Oil, divided
2 lg. Carrots, sliced
  diagonally
½ cup Cashews or Peanuts
Basmati Rice

Cut pork or chicken in thin strips. Set aside.

Heat 1 tbsp. Oil in large skillet over medium heat. Add carrots and celery, stir fry about 3 minutes.   Remove veggies and set aside.

Pour remaining oil into skillet, add meat and fry 3 minutes. Add veggies, honey, terriyaki sauce and nuts.   Cook until sauce starts to boil. Serve over hot basmati rice.

Occasion _____ Date _____

Comments _____

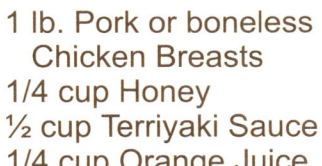

Pepper Steak with Potatoes

4 medium Potatoes, sliced
  1/4" thick
1 lb. London broil, thinly
  sliced

1 tbsp. Garlic pepper
2 tbsp. Olive oil
1 gr. Bell Pepper, cut
  into thin strips
Salt and pepper to taste

Microwave potatoes 6 - 10 minutes or until tender. Toss beef and garlic pepper.

Heat oil in large skillet over high heat. Add beef and toss 3 minutes. Remove beef. Add green pepper and toss 3 minutes. Add potatoes and saute 5 minutes. Add beef, toss until heated through.

Serves 4.

Occasion _____ Date _____

Comments _____

Helpful Hint   To keep fruit cakes moist while baking, place a pan of water alongside it in oven, and keep replacing the water until the cake is done.

Sophisticated Garlic Chicken

2 tbsp. Flour
1/4 tsp. Pepper
2 heads Garlic,
    separated into cloves
    and peeled

4 Chicken Breasts, skinned
1 tbsp. Oil
1 cup Chicken Stock
½ cup Balsamic Vinegar
½ cup Thyme

In a plastic bag, combine flour and half the pepper. Add chicken and shake to coat. In Dutch oven, heat oil and brown chicken. Transfer to a plate.

Add garlic and any remaining flour to pan. Cook, stirring 2 minutes. Add stock, vinegar, thyme and remaining pepper. Bring to a boil, scraping up bits. Simmer over medium heat 5 minutes. Pour over browned chicken and serve or strain, and use as a sauce.

Return chicken to pan, cover and cook 20 - 25 minutes longer.

Occasion _____ Date _____

Comments _____

Roast Duck

3 Ducks, dressed
3 tsp. Soy Sauce
½ cup low sugar
    Orange Marmalade

6 Bacon strips
3 small Onions, chopped
1 stalk Celery, chopped
½ tsp. Garlic powder

Put 1 tsp. soy sauce, onion and celery in each duck. With ducks in roasting pan, sprinkle with salt, pepper and garlic powder. Top with the marmalade and place 2 bacon strips on each duck. Cover and roast in 370F. oven for 1 hour.

Allow to rest 20 minutes. Then slice and serve. Discard bacon. Make sauce on drippings.

Occasion _____ Date _____

Comments _____

 Tip To control mice, leave container of peppermint extract wherever you suspect the mice are entering.

Succulent Pork Roast

1 X 3 lb. boneless Pork Loin
2 cloves Garlic, thinly sliced
2 tbsp. Dijon Mustard
1 tsp. Red Wine Vinegar
  or Balsamic Vinegar
3/4 tsp. fresh Thyme
½ tsp. fresh Sage

3/4 cup Beef Broth
3/4 cup unsweetened
  Apple Juice
1/4 cup Apricot Jam
1 ½ cups Apples, peeled
  and chopped
1 tbsp. Sour Cream
1 tbsp. Cornstarch

Cut 8 deep slits in roast and insert garlic slices.

Mix together next four ingredients and brush over roast in roasting pan.

Mix together juice, broth and jam over medium heat until melted. Pour over roast.

Arrange chopped apples around roast. Reserve ½ cup apples. Cook in 350F. oven for 1 1/4 ~ 1 ½ hours, basting at ½ hour intervals. When done, remove roast. Rest 20 minutes.

Skim off fat from pan juices, then add remaining ½ cup apples. Mix in sour cream until smooth. Bring in cornstarch and cook until bubbly.

Slice roast in thin slices, pouring gravy over the platter. Decorate with sprigs of sage.

Serves 8 - 10.

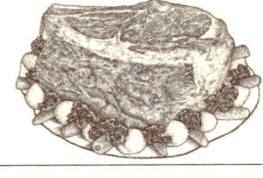

Occasion _____ Date _____

Comments _____

_____

_____

Lighter Fare What lies at the bottom of the ocean and twitches? A nervous wreck!

Roast Beef Tip & Vegetables

1 X 4 lb. boneless
   Top Sirloin Roast
1 tsp. Salt
1 tbsp. Flour
1 tsp. Oil
1 ½ cups Barbecue
   Sauce
1 ½ cup low sodium
   Beef Broth
1/4 cup Worcestershire
   Sauce

4 medium White Potatoes,
   cut in half lengthwise
½ Turnip, cut lengthwise
3 cloves Garlic, minced
1 tsp. Dry Mustard
1/4 tsp. Black Pepper
2 tbsp. Lime Juice
2 small heads Cabbage,
   cut in 8 wedges
20 Pearl Onions, peeled
4 medium Sweet Potatoes,
   cut in half lengthwise

Preheat oven to 350F.

Sprinkle flour with salt and roll meat on all sides well. Then add oil to roasting pan and brown roast.

In a medium bowl, combine barbecue sauce, worcestershire sauce, garlic, mustard, black pepper, lime juice and beef broth. Mix well. Pour over roast. Cook covered 1 hour. Reduce oven to 325F. and cook another hour. Baste often.

Remove roasting pan, arrange vegetables around roast. Cover and roast another hour.

Remove roast and allow to stand 15 minutes before carving. Slice thinly, place on platter, and add vegetables around.

Use remaining drippings in pan for sauce for meat. Serves 8.

Occasion _____ Date _____
Comments _____
_____

Helpful Hint To stop creamer from dripping, put a dab of butter under the spout.

Roast Turkey with Cranberry Stuffing

1 loaf Italian or French
   Bread, torn into cubes
2 tbsp. Butter
1 ½ cups chopped Onions
1 ½ cups chopped Celery
3 tsp. fresh chopped Sage
1 tsp. dried Thyme leaves
½ tsp. fresh Rosemary,
   chopped

1/4 tsp. Salt
½ cup chopped Walnuts
1/4 tsp. Black Pepper
1 ½ cups coarsely chopped
   fresh Cranberries
1 tbsp. Sugar
3/4 cup Chicken Broth
1 X 8-10 lb. Turkey

Preheat oven to 375F.   Spread bread on cookie sheet and toast in oven for 12 minutes.   Reduce oven to 350F.

Melt butter in large saucepan, add onions and celery and cook until tender.   Remove and add bread, sage, thyme, rosemary, salt, pepper and nuts.   Mix well.

Mix together cranberries and sugar and add to bread. Mix.   Drizzle chicken broth.   Mix together well.

Prepare turkey and stuff loosely.   Place remaining stuffing in a casserole dish sprayed with cooking oil.   Put turkey on rack in roasting pan, breast side up.   Loosely tent with foil and cook 3 hours.

Allow turkey to rest before carving.   During this time, cook remaining stuffing at 375F. for 20 - 30 minutes. Serves 20.

Occasion _____ Date _____

Comments _____

△ Tip   Great Spirit, help me never to judge another until I have walked in his moccasins for two weeks.

Rack of Lamb with Pesto / Mustard Crust

2 slices White Bread, cut in quarters	7 tbsp. Dijon Mustard
2 lg. Garlic cloves	2 X 14.5 oz. cans Beef Broth
2 tbsp. fresh Rosemary	3 tbsp. Unsalted Butter
2 tbsp. fresh Thyme	½ cup Pesto Sauce
1 tbsp. Olive oil	2 well trimmed racks of Lamb, 1 ½ lbs. each

Pesto Sauce:

Place 1 clove of garlic, 1 tsp. sea salt, 1 tbsp. pine nuts, 2 tsp. walnut pieces, ½ cup basil leaves and ½ cup olive oil in a processor. Transfer to bowl and stir in 2 tbsp. grated parmesan cheese.

Preheat oven to 425F.

Combine white bread, garlic, rosemary and thyme in processor until finely chopped.

Heat olive oil in an ovenproof skillet and brown lamb about 7 minutes. Remove lamb and coat with breadcrumb mixture. Season with salt and pepper and return to skillet, roasting until cooked ~ 35 minutes for medium-rare. Transfer lamb to cutting board and rest.

Pour fat from skillet out, add beef broth, boiling to reduce by half ~ 8 minutes. Whisk in butter. Cut meat into chops. Pour sauce over lamb, serving lamb drizzled with pesto sauce. Serves 6.

Occasion _____ Date _____

Comments _____

_____

Lighter Fare A family of 3 tomatoes were walking one day when baby tomato started lagging behind. Father tomato walks back to her, stomps on her, squashing her into red paste, and says, "Ketchup!"

Pork Chops with Sauce

6 Loin Pork Chops
6 cloves Garlic, minced
2 tsp. shredded Ginger
1 tbsp. Butter
1 tbsp. Olive Oil
2 tbsp. Cider Vinegar

2 tbsp. Cold Butter, cubed
1 cup Carrots, sliced in
  rounds
1 cup sliced Turnip
1 cup diced Apples
2 tbsp. Raisins, plumped
½ cup Apple Cider

Sear or brown chops in frying pan with oil and butter.

In a 2 qt. Baking dish, greased, mix vegetables, apples, raisins, garlic and ginger.   Place on bottom, then layer chops on top.   Drizzle cider vinegar over top with salt and pepper to taste.   Cover and cook in 350F. oven for 1 hour.   Place chops and vegetables together on platter.

Sauce:
To remaining drippings, add juice from plumped raisins and ½ cup cider.   When boil is reached, whisk in cold butter. Strain or leave as is. Serves 6.

Occasion _____ Date _____

Comments _____
_____
_____
_____

Helpful Hint To deodorize your microwave, place a bowl of water with 6 lemon slices added to it. Cook on high for approximately 30 seconds.

Buttermilk Chicken

8 slices Rye Bread
1 cup Buttermilk
1 tsp. Hot Pepper Sauce
4 lbs. Chicken pieces

Salt and Pepper
3/4 cup grated Parmesan
   Cheese
1 tsp. dried Thyme

Preheat oven to 400F. Generously grease with oil a baking sheet. Pulse the bread in a processor into coarse crumbs.

Mix together on a flat pie plate buttermilk, hot pepper sauce, 3/4 tsp. salt and ½ tsp. Pepper.   On another plate, mix breadcrumbs, parmesan cheese, thyme and 1/8 tsp. pepper.

Place chicken in buttermilk mixture, turning to coat evenly, working one piece at a time. Dredge in breadcrumb mixture, coating evenly and place on prepared baking sheet. Bake until golden brown ~ 35 minutes.

Leave enough space between pieces so they crisp evenly. Serve 6.

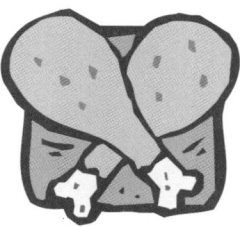

Occasion _____ Date _____

Comments _____

_____

_____

_____

 Tip May the warm winds of heaven blow gently on this house; may the Great Spirit, our Creator, bless all who enter here.

Real Native Supper

3 Pork Hocks
1 Onion, minced
3 Carrots, chopped
   in rounds
6 Potatoes, halved

4 cups Chicken stock
3 stalks Celery, cut
   in half
Salt and Pepper

Place hocks in large pot covered with 4 cups chicken stock, onion and celery. Let simmer for 3 hours.

Add salt and pepper and other veggies. Cook until veggies are tender. Remove and serve together on large platter. Save remaining liquid as stock for a hearty winter soup or stew.

Occasion _____ Date _____
Comments _____
_____

Turkey Supreme

2 tbsp. Butter
½ cup Sugar
1 tsp. grated Orange
   Peel
2 cups fresh Cranberries
5 cups leftover Turkey
1 cup Turkey Stock

1 cup Milk
1 tsp. Salt
1/4 tsp. Pepper
2 tbsp. Onion, finely chopped
2 cups soft Breadcrumbs
   or leftover stuffing
2 Eggs, slightly beaten

Melt butter in 8" baking pan. Blend sugar and orange peel with cranberries and cover bottom of pan.
Combine remaining ingredients and mix well. Fill up pan.
Bake at 400oF. for 45 minutes. Turn out on platter upside down. Serve hot. Serves 8.

Occasion _____ Date _____
Comments _____
_____

Lighter Fare What did the left eye say to the right eye? "Between us, something smells good; they must be cooking from the Medley of First Nations Cooking!"

Cider Glazed Ham

½ fully cooked Smoked
  Ham (not spiral cut)
3/4 cup packed light
  Brown Sugar

1/4 cup Dijon Mustard
3 tbsp. Cider
1/4 cup Red Currant Jelly

Preheat oven to 350F. Trim all but 1/4" fat from ham and score remaining into 1/4" diamonds without cutting into meat.   Place in roasting pan on a rack.

Mix together in bowl brown sugar, cider, mustard and red currant jelly. Brush over ham. Bake ham brushing glaze every 30 minutes until gone ~ 2 hours. Let ham stand 15 minutes before carving.

Serves 12.

Occasion _____ Date _____
Comments _____
_____
_____

Broiled Deer Steaks

4 steaks cut 1" thick

Put steaks in a broiling rack about 3" from coals, 2 to 3 minutes per side.

Serve with salt and pepper.   Can do buffalo steaks the same way.

Occasion _____ Date _____
Comments _____
_____
_____

 **Helpful Hint** To freshen up thermos bottles, fill them with warm water mixed with 2 tbsp. of baking soda.

Cranberry Sauce

1 lb. fresh Cranberries,
  washed
1 cup Maple Syrup

1 cup Sugar
1 1/4 cups Water

Place all ingredients in a large saucepan, bringing to a boil. Reduce heat and simmer for about 20 minutes, or until cranberries pop.

Cool and serve.

Occasion ——————————————— Date ———————
Comments ————————————————————————————
————————————————————————————————————

Spiced Crabapples

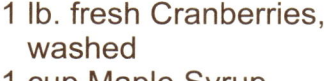

Crabapples
1 qt. Vinegar
4 cups Sugar
1 tbsp. Mace

1 tbsp. Allspice
1 Cinnamon Stick
1 tbsp. Whole Cloves

Wash and remove blossom end of firm crabapples.   Do not peel.

Mix vinegar, spices and sugar. Boil until syrup coats a spoon. Add apples, reheat mixture slowly to avoid bursting the skins, and simmer until apples are tender.

Pack into clean sterile hot jars. Cover with hot syrup and seal.

Occasion —————————————————— Date ——————
Comments ————————————————————————————
————————————————————————————————————

 Tip   "May the sun shine warmly upon you, the wind blow gently upon your face, a rainbow always touch your shoulder, and the moccasins of your life leave good trails." RWM

Marvellous Meat Dishes

Favourite Recipes from Family Members and Friends
(Recipes can be written in or pasted on)

Marvellous Meat Dishes

Favourite Recipes from Family Members and Friends
(Recipes can be written in or pasted on)

M
A
R
V
E
L
L
O
U
S

M
E
A
T

D
I
S
H
E
S

SCRUMPTIOUS GASTRIC MEMORIES

My Favourite Cook

Prize Winning Photo

Christmas Time

Favourite Family Foto

FOOD FUN FOTOS

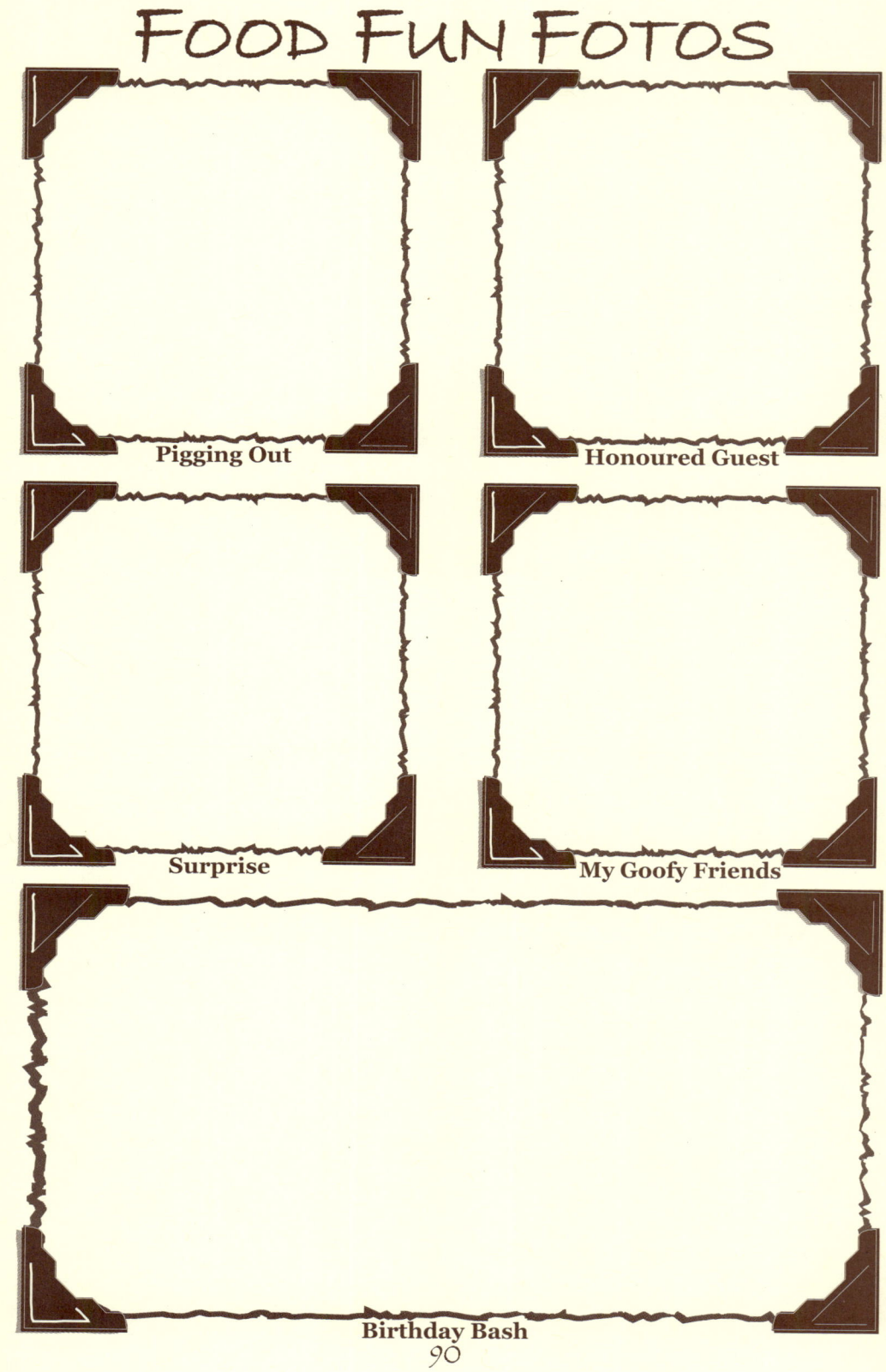

Pigging Out

Honoured Guest

Surprise

My Goofy Friends

Birthday Bash

PowWow Fare

Indian Tacos

Topping:
1 lb. fried Hamburger
2 cans Tomatoes
1 lg. Green Pepper
1 lg. Onion

Mushrooms
½ cup cooked Rice
1 sm. can Refried Beans
1 lg. can Red Kidney Beans
1 tsp. Chili Spice
Few drops Tabasco Sauce

PowWows are famous for tacos. A whole family could feed off one!

Fry Bread:
4 cups white Flour

½ tsp. Salt
1 tbsp. Baking Powder

Combine all ingredients. Add about 1 ½ cups lukewarm water and knead until dough is soft but not sticky. Shape dough into balls the size of a small peach. Shape in to patties by hand. Dough should be about ½ inch thick.

Make a small hole in the centre of the round. Fry one at a time in about 1 inch hot lard or shortening in a heavy pan. Brown on both sides. Drain on paper towels.

Occasion _____ Date _____

Comments _____

_____

 Lighter Fare One Sunday morning the pastor noticed a young man staring at a plaque hanging in the church foyer. The young man said, 'Good morning, Pastor' not taking his eyes off the plaque, asked, 'What is this?' The pastor answered, 'These are all the people who have died in the service.' Soberly the two stood there before the plaque and after a long silence the young man asked, 'Which service sir, the 8:30 or the 10:30?'

Traditional Iroquois Dried Corn Soup

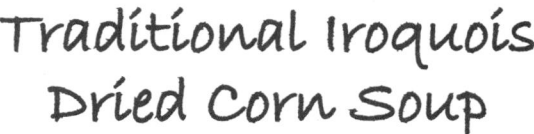

Soup pot full of water
2 - 3 Pork Hocks (or your
   choice of meat)
2 cups dried Corn

3 cans white Navy Beans
   or 1 small bag dried
   Navy Beans, cooked
   to package directions

Traditionally, sweet corn was cut off the cob and dried in the sun until all moisture was removed. This made it easy to transport and save. Now, we speed up this process by drying the corn in the oven at 350F. And stirring often. This process takes approximately 1 ½ hours depending on your oven. Many people dry a lot during harvest time and make this soup all winter.

Boil water and meat for 2 to 3 hours. Take meat off bone and put back in pot of broth.

Add to meat and broth the dried corn and navy beans, simmering for 2 hours before serving.

This soup is always better the second day and freezes well.

Our oldest daughter, Rachel's favourite soup!

Occasion _____ Date _____
Comments _____
_____

Helpful Hint The Sunday School teacher asks Johnny, "Tell me, do you say your prayers before eating?" "No," Johnny replies, "I don't have to, my mom's a good cook!"

Navajo Burrito

1 lbs. lean Ground Beef
1 Onion, chopped
2 Garlic Cloves, chopped
2 tsp. Soy Sauce

1 Bell Pepper, red, diced
1 can chopped Green Chilies
1 ½ cup frozen Sweet Corn
1 can Black Beans
1 can diced Tomatoes
1 cup Chicken Stock
½ cup Instant Rice

Cook first four ingredients together. Add pepper, chilies, corn, beans and tomatoes and cook further 15 minutes.

Add chicken stock and rice and simmer 5 minutes. Set aside.

2 cups shredded Cheese
Package of large Tortillas

In frying pan with teaspoon of oil coating pan, get very hot and brown tortillas for 1 minute on each side.

Take tortilla, spoon mixture into middle and sprinkle with shredded cheese. Wrap and serve with salsa or sour cream.

*Our daughter, Rebecca, says these are great!
Her family developed a craving for spice from
living in Arizona for awhile.*

Occasion _____ Date _____
Comments _____
_____
_____

 Tip   By the time you can make ends meet,
they move the ends.

Wild Rice Side Dish

2 cups Wild Rice
½ cup Celery, chopped
½ cup Onion, finely
   chopped
3 tbsp. Oil

Salt & Pepper
2 Carrots, diced
4 tbsp. Butter
4 cups Chicken broth
1/4 cup each Walnuts,
   Raisins

Saute rice in butter and oil to cook on all sides.

Add celery, carrots and onions to broth.   Simmer covered for about 45 minutes.   Check to see when rice becomes plump. Remove from heat and add nuts, raisins, salt and pepper.   Serve hot as a side dish to pork or chicken.

Occasion _____ Date _____

Comments _____

_____

_____

_____

Lighter Fare A preacher stoped beside a car that was turned over on its side in the ditch. He climbed up on the car and yelled, "Are you alright in there?" "Yes," came the reply, "I've got an angel riding with me," to which the preacher replied, "You better let him ride with me. You'll get him killed."

Fry Bread

4 cups White Flour
½ tsp. Salt
1 tbsp. Baking Powder

Combine all ingredients. Add about 1 ½ cups lukewarm water and knead until dough is soft but not sticky. Shape dough into balls the size of a small peach. Shape into patties by hand. The dough should be about ½ inch thick.

Make a small hole in the centre of the round. Fry one at a time in about 1 inch of hot lard or shortening in a heavy pan. Brown on both sides. Drain on paper towels and serve hot with honey or jam.

Occasion _____ Date _____
Comments _____
_____
_____
_____

 Tip   Things you never hear said in church . . .
1. It's my turn to sit on the front pew.
2. I find this service more enjoyable than golf.
3. I love singing hymns I've never heard of.
4. Since we're all here, let's start early.
5. I was so thrilled, and never noticed your sermon went
     25 minutes overtime.

PowWow Fare

Favourite Recipes from Family Members and Friends
(Recipes can be written in or pasted on)

**P
O
W
W
O
W

F
A
R
E**

PowWow Fare

Favourite Recipes from Family Members and Friends
(Recipes can be written in or pasted on)

P
O
W
W
O
W

F
A
R
E

Sassy Salads

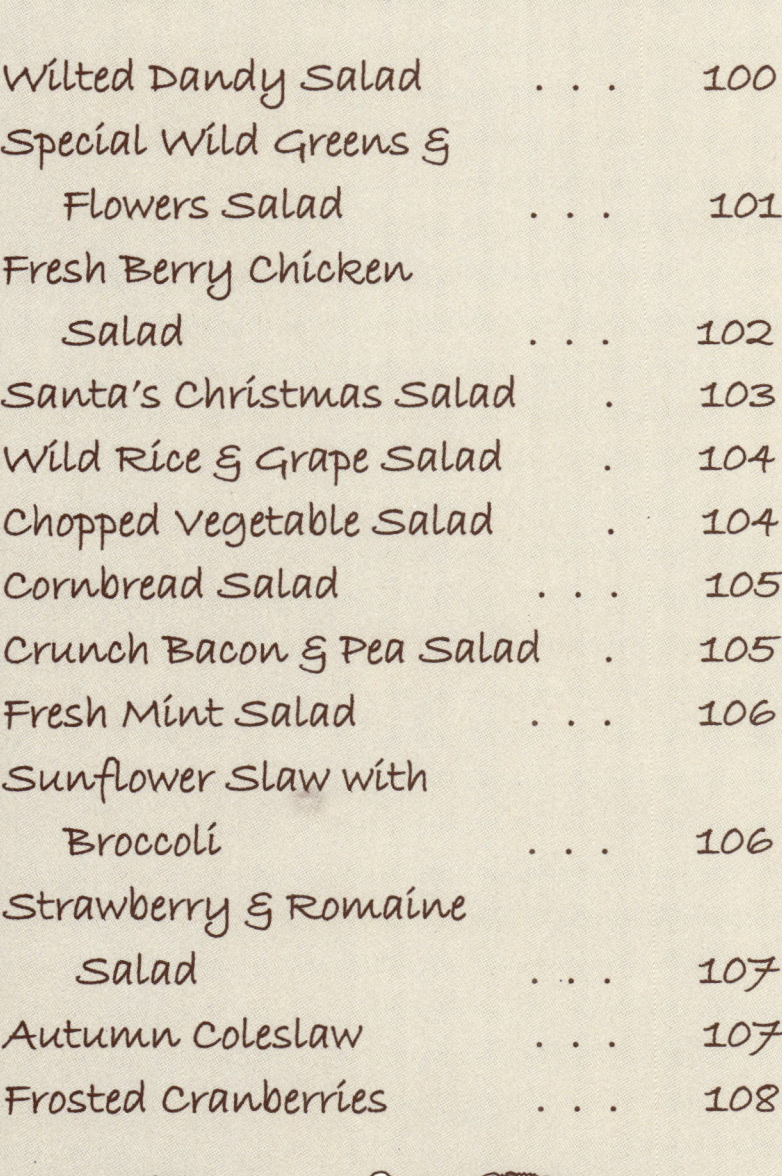

SASSY SALADS

Wilted Dandy Salad

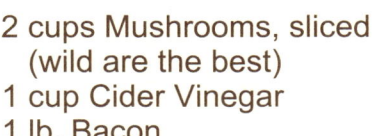

2 cups Mushrooms, sliced
   (wild are the best)
1 cup Cider Vinegar
1 lb. Bacon
Salt and Pepper

2 lg. brown bags of
   Dandelion Greens,
   raw and cleaned
1 cup Water
3 tbsp. Sugar

Cook bacon in a 5 quart iron skillet. Leave drippings and remove bacon.

Add cider vinegar, sugar, water and seasonings. Bring to boil.

Add mushrooms to greens and pour dressing over greens and mix well. Serves 12.

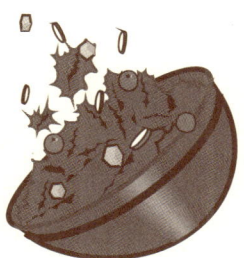

Occasion _____ Date _____
Comments _____
_____
_____
_____

Helpful Hint To clean sink drain, pour ½ cup baking soda
followed by a cup of vinegar down the drain.
Let the mixture foam, then run hot water.

Special Wild Greens & Flowers Salad

1 cup Watercress leaves
1 cup Lamb's Quarter
  new leaves (or small
  Spinach leaves)
1 cup Arugula lettuce,
  torn to bite size pieces
½ cup tender Nasturtium
  and Violet leaves, torn up

1/4 cup Cider Vinegar
1/3 cup Salad oil
2 tsp. Fresh Mint, fine &
  bruised (use as much
  mint leaves as you like)
2 tsp. chopped fresh
  Tarragon
Salt & Pepper to taste

Salads in the Spring use new, tender greens. All salads are flavoured by herbs. They made oil pressed from seeds and especially used with a vinegar made from fermented, evaporated, uncooked maple sap. This is a recipe of a Spring tonic salad beloved by all woodland people after the long winters.

Dressing:
  Combine honey and vinegar, whisking in oil. Whisk in crushed mint. Season to taste with salt. Pour over greens and flowers in large bowl. Toss well. Serve immediately.

Occasion _____ Date _____
Comments _____
_____
_____
_____

 Tip   *A balanced diet is a cookie in each hand!*
        Tim's motto: RWM

Fresh Berry Chicken Salad

8 cups torn Mixed Greens or Organic Greens

1 lb. Boneless Chicken Breast, cooked and cut into strips

2 cups assorted Berries (blue raspberries, strawberries)

1 8 oz. pkg. frozen Sugar Snap Peas

1/4 cup toasted Pecans or slivered Almonds

Dressing:
Orange Balsamic Vinaigrette

½ cup Orange Juice
1 tbsp. Sugar
½ cup Balsamic Vinegar

½ cup Olive Oil
Salt and Pepper

Put above ingredients in a bottle and shake well. Tweak on tasting as it may need more sugar or juice. Salt and pepper to taste.

Occasion _____ Date _____
Comments _____
_____
_____
_____

Lighter Fare   Two heavily perspiring men on a tandem bicycle finally got to the top of the hill. "Wow," said the first man, "It was an unbelievable climb." "It certainly was," replied the second man. "And if I hadn't kept the brake on, we probably would have slid down backwards."

Santa's Christmas Salad

1/4 cup red Cinnamon
   Candy
3 tbsp. Sugar
1 pkg. Flavoured
   Cherry Gelatin Mix
1/4 cup Nuts

1 cup Mayonnaise
1 cup cold Water
1 cup hot Water
1 cup diced Apples
½ cup diced Oranges

Dissolve candy and sugar in hot water. Heat just to boiling, pour over jello and dissolve. Add cold water. Add red food colouring, if desired for a brighter colour. Chill until partially set.

Stir in remaining ingredients. Pour into oiled large or Santa shaped mould. Chill until firm

Serve using mayonnaise and accent hair, beard and fur of mould. Serves 6.

Occasion _____ Date _____

Comments _____

_____

_____

_____

 No "curly" bacon for breakfast
when you dip it into cold water before frying.

Wild Rice & Grape Salad

3 cups cooked
   Wild Rice
1 cup seedless Green
   Grapes, halved
1 small can Water
   Chestnuts, sliced

½ cup Celery, chopped
   medium fine
1 big bunch Green Onions,
   chopped medium fine
½ cup slivered and
   sliced Almonds
1 cup Mayonnaise
   (must be Hellman's)

Stir vegetables and mayonnaise into rice.   Stir grapes in gently.   If too thick, thin with a little milk.   Taste for seasoning.

Keep refrigerated.   Better to make a day ahead. Flavours meld better.

Chopped Vegetable Salad

½ lb. Green Beans and
½ lb. Yellow Beans, blanched,
   cooled and cut diagonally
Red Onion, chopped
1 Cucumber, chopped
Red & Green Peppers,
   chopped
Small Tomato, seeded and
   chopped

Cilantro, chopped
2 ears Corn, cooked,
   cut off cob
1 Jalapeno Pepper for heat
Salt and Pepper to taste
1 cup Peas
1 can Black Beans
Red Wine Vinegar
Olive Oil

Shake together red wine vinegar, olive oil, salt and pepper. Mix salad ingredients and set for 1 hour.   Top with vinaigrette.

Occasion _____ Date _____

Comments _____
_____

Lighter Fare   Why don't blind people like to skydive?
Because the "seeing eye dog goes crazy."

Cornbread Salad

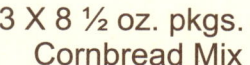

3 X 8 ½ oz. pkgs.
  Cornbread Mix
6 - 8 Radishes, thinly
  sliced
3 Tomatoes, chopped

1 Green Pepper,
  chopped
1 bunch chopped
  Green Onions

Make cornbread and cool. Crumble bread in large bowl, adding all vegetables. Pour dressing over top 15 minutes before serving. Serves 6.

Dressing:
1 cup Cucumber
  Dressing

3/4 cup Mayonnaise
3 tbsp. Mustard

Blend together until well blended and creamy.

Occasion _____ Date _____
Comments _____

Crunchy Bacon & Pea Salad

4 slices Bacon,
  crispy & crumbled
3 Green Onions, sliced
  diagonally
1 stalk Celery, diced

10 oz. pkg. frozen
  Peas, thawed
1/4 cup Mayonnaise
1/4 cup Sour Cream
1/4 tsp. Salt
1/8 tsp. Pepper

Combine all ingredients together. Chill before serving. Serves 6.

Occasion _____ Date _____
Comments _____

Tip One honey dipped cruller consists of 11 grams of fat, the amount of consuming 11 slices of whole wheat toast.

Fresh Mint Salad

2 cups chopped Watercress
2 cups chopped Romaine
1 cup diced Radishes
4 Green Onions sliced in
   half lengthwise & chopped
½ cup chopped Mint, fresh

Place greens in large bowl.

Mix dressing ingredients together. For best flavour, dressing can be made 2 hours ahead of time.

Pour over greens and toss. Let stand 10 minutes and toss again. Serves 6 - 8.

Dressing:
½ cup Salad Oil
1/4 cup Tarragon
   Vinegar
1 tsp. Salt
1/4 tsp. Pepper

Occasion _____ Date _____

Comments _____

_____

Sunflower Slaw with Broccoli

16 oz. pkg. Broccoli
   Slaw mix
2 bunches Green Onions,
   chopped
2 X 3oz. pkgs. Ramen
   Noodles with seasoning,
   uncooked
½ cup slivered Almonds
1/3 cup White Vinegar
½ cup Sugar
½ cup Sunflower Seeds
1 cup Oil

Mix together broccoli slaw and onions. Break ramen noodles and toss with slaw mix. Set aside.

Combine noodle seasoning, vinegar, sugar and oil over slaw. Let stand at least 2 hours.

Just before serving, stir in sunflower seeds and almonds. Serves 4 - 6.

Occasion _____ Date _____

Comments _____

_____

⚠ **Tip** One honey dipped cruller consists of 11 grams of fat, the amount of consuming 11 slices of whole wheat toast.

Strawberry & Romaine Salad
with Banana Poppyseed Dressing

2 cups Romaine Lettuce, torn
2 tbsp. Red Onion, chopped

3/4 cup sliced
   Strawberries

Mix together.   Serves 1 - 2.

Dressing:
1 Banana, mashed
1 cup Sour Cream
1/4 cup Sugar

1 tbsp. Poppy Seeds
1 tbsp. Lemon Juice
1 tsp. Dry Mustard
3/4 tsp. Salt

Blend together and chill 30 minutes.   Makes 3 cups.

Occasion _____ Date _____
Comments _____
_____

Autumn Coleslaw

2 ½ cups Red and Green
   Cabbage, shredded together
3/4 cup shredded Carrots
3/4 cup Red and Green Sweet
   Peppers, julienned
1/4 cup sliced Onion
½ cup Raisins or Grape halves

1/3 cup fat-free Salad
   Dressings
1 tbsp. Vinegar
1 tbsp. Skim Milk
1/4 tsp. Celery Seed
1/4 tsp. fresh Dill

In a large bowl mix vegetables together.
In a small bowl mix 5 last ingredients to make dressing.
Pour dressing over vegetables and mix gently to coat.
Chill and serve. Serves 6.

Occasion _____ Date _____
Comments _____
_____

Lighter Fare   I think my wife is getting tired of me.
She keeps wrapping my lunches in roadmaps.

Frosted Cranberries

2 cups fresh Cranberries
2 cups unpeeled Apples
1 cup Sugar

2 cups mini Marshmallows
1 cup whipped Cream
1 cup Pecans

Grind cranberries and cored apples.   Add sugar and let stand 30 minutes.

Add marshmallows and let stand 1 hour.

Fold in cream and nuts.   Freeze, if desired.

Occasion _____ Date _____

Comments _____
_____
_____
_____

Helpful Hint   To remove lime deposits from tea kettles,
fill with equal parts of vinegar and water.
Bring to a boil and let sand overnight.

Sassy Salads

Favourite Recipes from Family Members and Friends
(Recipes can be written in or pasted on)

S
A
S
S
Y

S
A
L
A
D
S

SASSY SALADS

Favourite Recipes from Family Members and Friends
(Recipes can be written in or pasted on)

**S
A
S
S
Y

S
A
L
A
D
S**

Sensational Soups

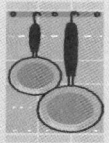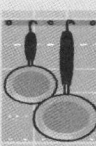

Mohawk Corn Soup

2 qts. Hominy corn
10 qts. Water from stock
1 tsp. Wood Ashes (black
   ash is the best)

2 cups Beans
1 cup chopped Saltpork
   or 2 large Pork Hocks or
   Chicken (meat removed
   from bone)

Preparing Hominy Corn:

   The corn used is white flour corn, dried on the cob and when dried, shelled by hand. The corn is then lyed with wood ashes mixed with water and boiled. Black hulls will surface as it boils. Remove corn from heat, skim off hulls, drain and rinse well. Replace water and return to stove. Process should be repeated 3 or 4 times until kernels start to puff up. At this stage it will look like hominy, but not broken up. You are ready to make soup.

   Cook in another pot your stock with chosen meat until thoroughly cooked. Remove meat from bone.

   Red kidney beans or white navy beans are also cooked in water to add to stock. Add all ingredients together and simmer approximately 2 hours. Season with salt and pepper.

   Serve with warm bread, homemade biscuits or bannock. Tastes better the second day!

Occasion _____ Date _____

Comments _____

_____

 Tip *One restaurant style egg roll consists of 6 grams of fat, the equivalent of eating 60 fresh peaches.*

Spring Chowder

1 tbsp. Margarine
4 cups Vidalia or
  Sweet Onions
1 cup chopped Celery
1 cup sliced Carrots
3 cups sliced Potato
  (1 1/4 pounds)
1 X 10.5 oz. low sodium
  Chicken Broth

1 cup Flour
2 cups 2% Milk
1/4 cup fresh Sage
Salt and Pepper
1 cup sliced Celery
1 chopped extra lean
  Ham
1/8 tsp. ground Nutmeg

Saute margarine, onions, carrots, celery and ham until tender. Add potatoes and broth, boiling slowly until potatoes are tender.

In small bowl mix flour and milk and add to pot. Salt and pepper to taste when chowder thickens. Add ground nutmeg and sage, cooking 2 more minutes. Serve piping hot. Garnish with sage leaves.

Spring Chowder was sold in the SkyDome PowWow to rave reviews. LJM

Serves 8.

Occasion _____ Date _____
Comments _____
_____
_____
_____

Lighter Fare   Put honey on your words ~ because if you have to eat them later, they'll taste good!

Hearty Beef Vegetable Soup

2 Bay leaves
1 lb. ground lean Beef
3 Carrots, chopped
2 cups shredded & chopped Cabbage
1 lg. can crushed Tomatoes

6 cups Beef Stock or Water
3 Potatoes, cubed
1 lg. Onion, chopped
3 stalks Celery, chopped
Any leftover veggies from night before

In a large heavy pot, cook hamburger until browned and add onions, celery and finish cooking. Add remaining ingredients and cook on simmer for the afternoon.

Skim off any fat that may settle on top. One hour before serving, add macaroni or barley or rice, if desired.

Serve piping hot with fresh baked bread or hot biscuits. Tastes great next day too! (if you have any left!)

Occasion _____ Date _____

Comments _____

_____

_____

_____

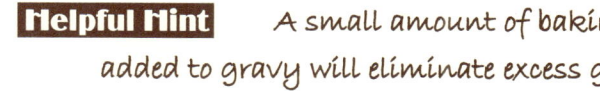

Helpful Hint A small amount of baking soda added to gravy will eliminate excess grease.

Creamy Corn Soup

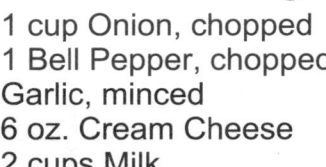

1 cup Onion, chopped	15 oz. can Creamed Corn
1 Bell Pepper, chopped	
Garlic, minced	15 oz. can Mushroom Soup
6 oz. Cream Cheese	
2 cups Milk	2 cups cooked Potatoes, cubed

With cooking spray, spray a large Dutch oven.   Add onion, bell pepper and garlic.   Saute 5 minutes.

Stir in cream cheese.   Reduce heat and cook until cheese is melted.

Add milk, corn and mushroom soup.   Add potatoes to rest of mixture, and heat through.

Remove from heat and garnish with crushed bacon bits.

Occasion _____ Date _____

Comments _____

_____

Iroquois Soup

4 lg. Mushrooms, sliced	½ tsp. Basil
2 X 10.5 oz. cans Beef Consomme	10 oz. Lima Beans
	1 Onion, chopped
2 tbsp. minced Parlsey	Green Pepper
2 tbsp. Cornmeal	1/4 tsp. Salt
1 clove crushed Garlic	12 oz. Haddock Fillets

Place mushrooms, consomme, cornmeal, parsley, garlic, basil, onion, salt and pepper in large saucepan. Simmer uncovered for 10 minutes.

Add haddock and lima beans and simmer for 20 minutes, stirring occasionally breaking haddock into bite-size pieces.   Serve hot.

Occasion _____ Date _____

Comments _____

_____

Tip   Finger-lickin' fried chicken is a fat attack! A typical takeout meal from a chicken food chain of 1 breast, 1 drumstick, coleslaw, fries and a biscuit will add to your growth with a dripping 1000 calories in fat.

Three Sisters Stew

1 tbsp. Olive Oil
1 lg. Onion, sliced
1 clove Garlic, crushed
1 Jalapeno Pepper,
  finely chopped
4 cups yellow summer
  Squash, sliced
4 cups Zucchini, cut
  into 1" pieces

4 cups Butternut Squash,
  peeled & cubed
3 cups Green Beans, cut
  into 1" pieces
1 cup frozen whole
  kernel Corn
1 tsp. Thyme leaves
2 X 16oz. cans Kidney
  Beans, undrained

Heat oil in Dutch oven over medium heat.   Cook onion, garlic and chili in oil for 2 minutes, stirring until onion is tender.

Stir in remaining ingredients.   Cook over low heat stirring until squash is tender.   Serves 6.

Occasion _____ Date _____
Comments _____
_____
_____
_____

Lighter Fare Refrigerate soups and broths before using them, allowing fat to rise to the top and solidify, and making it easier to remove.

Sensational Soups

Favourite Recipes from Family Members and Friends
(Recipes can be written in or pasted on)

Sensational Soups

Favourite Recipes from Family Members and Friends
(Recipes can be written in or pasted on)

S
E
N
S
A
T
I
O
N
A
L

S
O
U
P
S

Thirst Quenchers

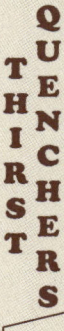

Tyendinaga Tea

1 cup dried Black Currants
1 cup dried Red Currants
½ cup chopped Raisins
1/4 cup Hibiscus Flowers dried
3 whole Cloves, broken up
1/8 cup Cranberries
½ cup dried Elderberries

Mix together and let meld for 24 hours.
Put 3 tbsp. Of mix in a pot of boiling water. Let steep for 7 minutes to burst the berries to freshness. Serve at a ladies function and you will have rave remarks.

Occasion _____ Date _____

Comments _____

Ginger Spice Tea

½ cup Sugar
2 slices Ginger
   or 1/4 tsp. Ginger
2 Cinnamon Sticks
1 tsp. whole Allspice

10 Tea Bags
4 cups boiling Water
8 cups cold Water
1 ½ cups Orange Juice

Pour boiling water over mixture and let steep 10 minutes. Strain solids from liquid. Add remaining ingredients. Refrigerate and serve over ice garnished with orange slices.

Occasion _____ Date _____

Comments _____

Lighter Fare   How do you get holy water?
You boil the hell out of it.

Lemonade

Make syrup of 1 cup sugar and 1 cup water. Make sure sugar is dissolved.

Take 1 lemon and cut in two. Add to pitcher of 1 qt. water, ice, 2 cups lemon juice and 1 cup syrup (made above). Mix well, and serve with piece of lemon rind on glass. Garnish with a piece of mint.

Occasion _____ Date _____

Comments _____

_____

Strawberry Refresher

½ cup crushed Strawberries
 and Juice
8 oz. Iced Water

2 tsp. Sugar Syrup
Fresh grated Nutmeg

In a 10 oz. glass place strawberries and sugar syrup. Blend well and add ice water together with a few ice cubes. Stir and top with a few grates of nutmeg.

Occasion _____ Date _____

Comments _____

Helpful Hint   To get rid of mildew stains, dab with hydrogen peroxide and launder as usual.

Wild Rose Flower Tea

Put 2 tbsp. dried Rose flowers per person in a cup and cover with boiling water, allowing to steep for 5 minutes.

Add sugar syrup (1 cup sugar dissolved in 1 cup warm water). Honey can also be used for added enhancing of flavour.

Note: Wild rose grows in thickets. Flowers are soft and delicate ~ 5 petalled pink or red.

Did you know the juice from rose hips is 25 times richer in Vitamin C than orange juice?

Rose petals or hips dried, and eaten raw, work as a stimulant when under heavy physical strain (used as a survival food).

Occasion _____ Date _____

Comments _____

_____

Mint Tea

10 lg. stalks fresh Mint, washed
2 qts. Spring Water

Place mint and water in large saucepan and bring slowly to boil. Turn off heat, cover and let steep 5 minutes. Strain and serve.

Occasion _____ Date _____

Comments _____

_____

Tip *To get rid of mildew stains, dab with hydrogen peroxide and launder as usual.*

Woodlands Berry Drink

1 cup Strawberries, cut up
1 cup Raspberries

1 cup dried Currants
1 cup Sugar
7 cups Water

Add 1 cup water to strawberries and raspberries. Add 1 cup hot water to dried currants. Let stand 1 hour
Mash each one to form pulp.
In a saucepan combine 1 cup sugar and 1 cup water to make a simple syrup.
Combine all fruits and add hot syrup and mix, adding in remaining water. Chill and serve, garnished with lemon and mint.

Occasion _____ Date _____
Comments _____

_____

Honey / Mint Drink

1 qt. Water
2/3 cups Honey

6 Mint leaves, torn

Place ingredients in container with lid. Shake well. Chill thoroughly and serve with ice, and garnish with mint.

Occasion _____ Date _____
Comments _____

_____

Lighter Fare Make a list of people who you need to get recipes from for your "Cookbook Heirloom": grandmother, mother, aunt, sister, etc.

Iced Dandelion Delight

1 tbsp. roasted Dandelion root	2 Cinnamon Sticks
1 tbsp. roasted Chicory Root	1 tsp. Vanilla
6 cups Water	2 - 3 tbsp. Honey
	Ice Cubes

Add dandelion root and chicory root to water in saucepan.   Add cinnamon sticks and bring to a simmer. Simmer 10 minutes then remove from heat.   Add vanilla and honey.

Cool and serve over ice for a refreshing drink.

Occasion _____ Date _____

Comments _____

_____

_____

_____

Helpful Hint   Tyendinaga Tea is one of the most satisfying tastes. As it is prepared, its fragrance fills the kitchen. The tea, prebagged, can be purchased through our office.

Thirst Quenchers

Favourite Recipes from Family Members and Friends

(Recipes can be written in or pasted on)

Thirst Quenchers

Favourite Recipes from Family Members and Friends

(Recipes can be written in or pasted on)

T H I R S T   Q U E N C H E R S

Vitalizing Veggies

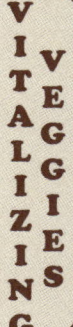

Potatoes, Beans & peas in Cream

2 lbs. small new Potatoes
Coarse Salt
12 oz. yellow or green
    Beans, trimmed & cut
    into 2" pieces

12 oz. fresh Peas
    in the pod
1 ½ cups heavy Cream
2 tbsp. unsalted Butter
Freshly ground Pepper

Place potatoes in medium saucepan and cover with water. Bring to a boil over high heat. Add salt. Reduce heat slowly and simmer until tender. Transfer to a medium bowl and cover loosely.

Place a steamer basket in a medium pot with about 2" of water.   Steam beans and peas until tender, about 5 to 6 minutes.

Combine cream and butter in a small saucepan and bring to a boil. Reduce heat to medium until thickened: 5 - 6 minutes.   Pour cream over vegetables and season with salt and pepper.   Toss to combine.

Occasion _____ Date _____
Comments _____
_____
_____
_____

Helpful Hint   During the rising stage of cooking bread, put in a cold oven, (not gas oven, or pilot light will dry out the bread). Put bowl of boiling water on rack beneath.

Succotash

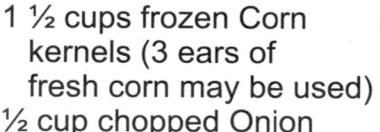

1 ½ cups frozen Corn kernels (3 ears of fresh corn may be used)
½ cup chopped Onion
1 cup chopped Summer Squash
1 cup chopped Red Bell Pepper
1 tsp. Cumin

1 tbsp. Olive oil
2 Garlic cloves, minced
½ cup defatted Chicken Broth
2 tbsp. chopped fresh Cilantro
1/8 tsp. Hot Sauce
1/8 tsp. Green Pepper
2 cups frozen Lima Beans, thawed

Place a large nonstick skillet over high heat until hot. Add corn, red pepper, onion and cumin. Saute 5 minutes until vegetables are slightly blackened.

Add summer squash, olive oil and garlic, sauteing an additional minute. Reduce heat to medium high, add broth and remaining ingredients. Cook 3 - 5 minutes, stirring frequently.

Occasion _____ Date _____
Comments _____
_____
_____
_____

▲ Tip   *"We long ago learned that some women are wiser than some men. If the women produced the Chief, she must be as wise as the Chief."* - Chief Red Cloud

Asparagus Cheese Tart

Flour for work surface
1 sheet frozen Puff Pastry
5½ oz. Gruyere Cheese,
  shredded (2 cups)

1 1/2 lb. medium thick
  Asparagus
1 tbsp. Olive Oil
Salt and Pepper

Preheat oven to 450F.

Flour surface and roll out pastry to a 16" X 10" rectangle. Place on a baking sheet. Score dough to 1" from the edge, making a rectangle shape. This ensures the middle won't puff up high during baking. Bake 15 minutes until golden.

Remove from oven and sprinkle cheese over rectangle part. Cut bottom of asparagus and with a potato peeler cut off tough outside skin and little tips. Put asparagus opposite ends to the tips. Brush with oil and season with salt and pepper. Bake until tender, about 20 to 25 minutes.

Occasion _____ Date _____

Comments _____

_____

_____

_____

Lighter Fare After church service a little boy told the pastor, "When I grown up, I'm going to give you some money." "Thank you," replied the pastor, "But why?" "Because, my dad says you're one of the poorest preachers we've had."

Scalloped Corn Bake

½ cup chopped Green Onion
1/4 cup chopped Red Pepper
1/4 cup chopped Green Pepper
2 tbsp. melted Butter

1 tsp. Salt
1 tbsp. Sugar
16 oz. cream style Corn
1 cup Cracker Crumbs
1 cup Milk
2 Eggs, slightly beaten
7 oz. whole Corn

Saute onions and peppers in butter until tender. Stir in remaining ingredients and pour into lightly greased baking dish.

Bake in preheated oven at 350F. for about 1 hour.

Occasion _____ Date _____
Comments _____

Turnip & Carrot Bake

2 lb. Carrots, cut into 2" long sticks
2 lb. Turnip, cut into 2" long sticks
1 tsp. Sugar   1/8 cup cubed Butter
2 tsp. Dill   Salt & Pepper

Mix all ingredients together and bake in a 350F. oven for 1 hour.

Occasion _____ Date _____
Comments _____

_____

Helpful Hint   To give your ice cream longer life in the freezer, cover container with aluminium foil.

Mashed Sweet Potatoes with Maple Syrup Kick

6 lb. Sweet Potatoes	2 tbsp. Maple Syrup
½ cup unsalted Butter	1 tsp. Salt
½ cup heavy Cream, heated	½ tsp. Black Pepper

Preheat oven to 400F.

Prick each potato twice with a fork and bake in a foil-lined shallow baking dish. Cook until tender, about 1 hour. Remove and cool slightly.

Halve potatoes lengthwise and scoop out warm flesh into a large bowl. Mash potatoes, stir in butter, cream, syrup, salt and pepper.

Drizzle lightly with maple syrup when serving.

Occasion _____ Date _____

Comments _____

_____

Asparagus with Blue Cheese

1 lb. Asparagus	3 slices Bacon, crisp
½ cup chopped Onion	2 tsp. Lemon Juice
½ cup Blue Cheese, crumbled	½ cup Walnuts, halved & toasted

Steam asparagus until cooked.

Fry bacon until crisp, then crumble.

Cook onion until tender. Stir in lemon juice, add asparagus. Cut diagonally the stalks into three pieces. Toss to coat. Heat through, add cheese and bacon. Heat until cheese melts. Sprinkle with walnuts.   Serves 4 - 6.

Occasion _____ Date _____

Comments _____

_____

Tip   To ease the pain and swelling of inflamed joints, apply a cooked onion directly on the sore spot.

Vitalizing Vegetables

Favourite Recipes from Family Members and Friends
(Recipes can be written in or pasted on)

V
I
T
A
L
I
Z
I
N
G

V
E
G
E
T
A
B
L
E
S

Vitalizing Vegetables

Favourite Recipes from Family Members and Friends
(Recipes can be written in or pasted on)

V
I
T
A
L
I
Z
I
N
G

V
E
G
E
T
A
B
L
E
S

Doggie Delights

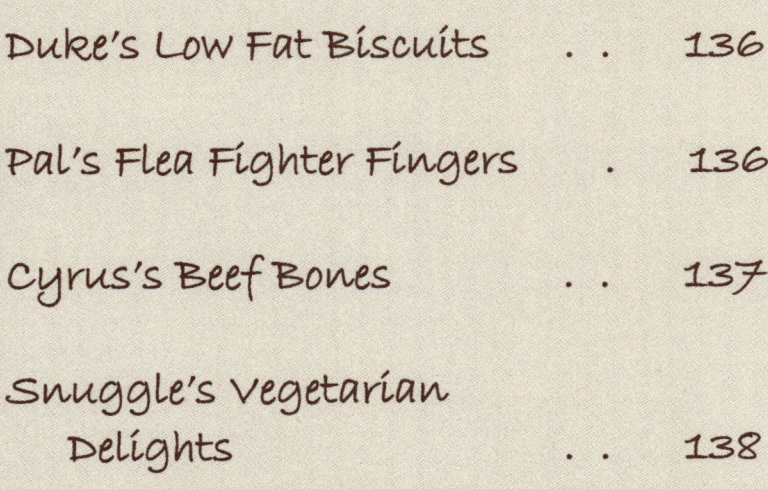

This section has been included because Natives love their dogs. These treats I have named after our long gone family pets.

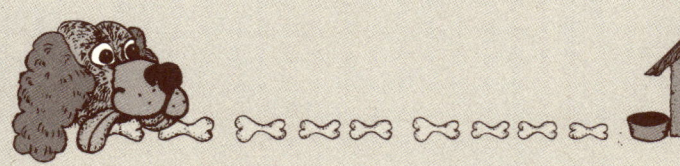

Duke's Low Fat Biscuits

2 cups Whole Wheat
  Flour
½ cup Flour
1/4 cup Cornmeal
2 Egg Whites
1/4 cup Skim Milk

1/4 cup Quick Oats
1 ½ tsp. Garlic Powder
2 tbsp. Vegetable Oil
1/4 cup Molasses
2 tbsp. cold Water

Combine flour, cornmeal, rolled oats and garlic powder.
Whisk separately oil, egg whites, molasses, milk and water.
Make a well in dry mixture, gradually adding liquid mixture.
Blend well.
  Divide dough into 2 balls. Knead each ball 2 minutes.
Roll out to ½" thickness. Cut biscuits, and place on baking
sheet. Bake 30 minutes in 350F. oven.   Turn off oven and
leave to harden for 1 hour. Makes about 50 biscuits.

Occasion _____ Date _____
Comments _____
_____

Pal's Flea Fighter Fingers

2 Beef Boullion Cubes
1 3/4 cups boiling Water
1 ½ cups Flour
1 ½ cups Whole Wheat Flour
1 cup Rye Flour
1 cup Cornmeal

1/4 cup Brewer's Yeast
2 tbsp. Garlic Powder
½ cup Oil
1 Egg, beaten
1 cup Rolled Oats

In a 2-cup measuring cup, dissolve cubes in boiling water.
Set aside.
  Mix dry ingredients. Make a well and add wet ingredients.
Blend well.
  Divide into 20 balls. Knead about 3 - 4 minutes. Roll out to
1/4 - ½". Cut and place on a foil-covered baking sheet. Bake
1½ hours at 300F.   Cool on a rack until hard, and store.
Tip: Brewer's Yeast helps pets repel fleas..

Occasion _____ Date _____
Comments _____
_____

Lighter Fare The four food groups: Fast, Frozen, Instant and Chocolate!

Cyrus's Beef Bones

1 lb. Ground beef   1 cup Quick Oats
2 Eggs, beaten   1 cup Water
3 cups Whole Wheat Flour

In a blender or food processor, combine meat and beaten eggs until well blended.   Set aside.

In a large bowl, combine flour and rolled oats. Gradually mix in beef mixture with hands until well blended.   Add water to form a sticky dough.

Divide into 2 balls.   Knead for 2 minutes adding enough flour until dough is no longer sticky.   Roll out and cut biscuits, placing on lightly greased or sprayed cookie sheet.   Bake for 1 hour at 350F.

Cook and store in dog's favourite container.   Great for gifts!   Makes 80 bones.

Occasion _____ Date _____

Comments _____

_____

_____

_____

Helpful Hint   Need a new game? Browse yard sales and flea markets for something different for your family to play together.

Snuggle's Vegetarian Delights

1 cup Quick Oats
1/4 cup Margarine
1 ½ cups hot Water
2 cloves Garlic, crushed
1 tbsp. Butter
1 X 250ml can Mixed
   Vegetables
Wash: 2 tbsp. Milk

½ cup Powdered Skim
   Milk
1 Egg, beaten
1 cup Cornmeal
1 cup Wheat Germ
21/2 cups Whole Wheat
   Flour
½ cup Rye Flour

In a large bowl combine rolled oats, margarine and hot water. Let stand 5 minutes.

In a frying pan, saute garlic in butter. Add garlic, milk and beaten eggs to rolled oats mixture. Stir until blended.

In a bowl combine cornmeal, wheat germ and flour. Gradually add flour mixture, ½ cup at a time. Blend well. Knead 3 - 4 minutes. Roll out to ½" cut cookies, and brush with milk.

Bake 1 hour in 300F. oven.   Cool and store.

Occasion _____ Date _____
Comments _____
_____
_____
_____

⚠ Tip   *"I am particularly fond of the little groves of oak trees. I love to look at them because they endure the winter storms and the summer's heat, and, not unlike ourselves, to see them flourish."*   - Chief Sitting Bull

Muffin's Mohawk Softies

for older dogs with missing teeth

1 pkg. Active Dry Yeast   1/4 cup warm Water
Pinch White Sugar   3 ½ cups Flour
2 Chicken Boullion Cubes   1 ½ cups Whole Wheat Flour
4 cups boiling Water   1 ½ cups Rye Flour
1 cup Cornmeal   ½ cup Skim Milk

Glaze:
1 Egg   2 tbsp. Milk

In a bowl dissolve yeast and sugar in warm water. Set aside.

In a medium bowl, combine flour, cornmeal and powdered skim milk.

Combine yeast and liquid mixture until well blended. Divide into 2 balls. Knead 1 minute. Roll to ½"or 1/4" thick. Place on foiled covered baking sheet. Whisk together egg and milk for a glaze.

Bake 25 minutes at 300F. Turn over after, and bake another 25 minutes.

Occasion _____ Date _____

Comments _____

_____

_____

_____

Lighter Fare After the christening service of his baby brother, little Johnny sobbed all the way home. His father asked him what was wrong. The boy replied, "That preacher said he wanted us brought up in a Christian home, and I want to stay with you guys."

Jasmine's Cheese Dreams

3 cups Whole Wheat Flour   1 cup shredded Cheese
2 tsp. Garlic Powder   1 Egg, beaten
½ cup Vegetable Oil   1 cup Milk

In a bowl dissolve yeast and sugar in warm water. Set aside.

In a medium bowl, combine flour, cornmeal and powdered skim milk.

Combine yeast and liquid mixture until well blended. Divide into 2 balls. Knead 1 minute. Roll to ½"or 1/4" thick. Place on foiled covered baking sheet.   Whisk together egg and milk for a glaze.

Bake 25 minutes at 300F.   Turn over after, and bake another 25 minutes.

Occasion _____ Date _____

Comments _____
_____
_____
_____

Tip "Children must learn early in life the beauty of generosity. They are taught to give what we prize most, that they may taste the happiness of giving."
- Mary Muktoyuk

Doggie Delights

Favourite Recipes from Family Members and Friends
(Recipes can be written in or pasted on)

DOGGIE DELIGHTS

Doggie Delights

Favourite Recipes from Family Members and Friends

(Recipes can be written in or pasted on)

**D
O
G
G
I
E

D
E
L
I
G
H
T
S**

Selected Menus
for Special Occasions

Children's Birthday Party

Kids love creating their own eats!

Courting

Christmas Menu

Mohawk Corn Soup . . . 112

Warm Acorn Bread . . . 32

Santa's Christmas Salad . . 103

Frosted Cranberries . . . 108

Roast Duck 77

Succotash 129

Mashed Sweet Potato with
    Maple Syrup Kick . . . 132

Baked Indian Pudding . . . 38

Sour Cream Raisin Pie . . 40

Business Lunch

Fresh Berry Chicken Salad . . 102

Wild Sage Bread 26

Wild Raspberry Bread
Pudding 41

Iced Dandelion Delight . . 124

Entertaining Friends

Cheese Dandelion Pate Loaf . . 20

Hot Onion & Chili Puffs . . 30

Special Wild Greens &
Flowers Salad . . . 101

Succulent Pork Roast . . . 78

Scalloped Corn Bake . . . 131

Turnip & Carrot Toss . . 131

Maple Upside Down Pudding . 40

Thanksgiving Dinner

Creamy Corn soup with
    Herbed Bread   . . .   115

Roast Turkey with
    Cranberry Stuffing   . . .   80

Chopped Vegetable Salad   . .   104

Asparagus Cheese Tart   . .   130

Turnip & Carrot Bake   . .   131

Rhubarb & Apple Crumble   . .   44

Sour Cream Raisin Pie   . .   40

My Personal Notes

My Personal Notes

Coming, Coming, Coming...

T • H • E   B • E • S • T
OF

BOTH WORLDS COOKBOOK

First Nations and Scottish

UNIQUE

&

COLLECTABLE

*This CookBook represents our
Prince Edward Island ancestry
with a "Rich Heritage of Recipes" reflecting
our Native and Scottish backgrounds.*

Ross & Linda Maracle
Tyendinaga Mohawks

My Personal Garden

First, plant four rows of . . .
   Presence
   Preparation
   Promptness
   Perseverance

Next, plant four rows of squash . . .
   Squash gossip
   Squash indifference
   Squash criticism
   Squash impatience

Then plant four rows of lettuce . . .
   Let us be faithful to our obligations
   Let us be loyal and unselfish
   Let us be diligent to duty
   Let us love one another

No garden is complete without turnips . . .
   Turn up with a smile
   Turn up with new ideas
   Turn up with encouragement
   Turn up with determination to . . .

"Remove the weeds and cultivate the good things that are growing in the 'Garden of My Life!'"

CONVENIENT ORDER FORMS

For order of 5 to 10 books, we'll pay the shipping to **one** address.   We offer attractive discounts on orders of 10 books or more. For details: **613-396-1435**
Email: *spiritalive@sympatico.ca*
Tremendous for Fundraising!

Please send ___ copies of *"Medley of First Nations Cooking"*
    at $19.95 each $_____

Postage & Handling: $3.00 for 1 book; $1.00 for
    each additional book (not applicable on orders
    of 5 to 10 books) $_____

                           Total enclosed $_____

Enclosed is my ☐ Cheque ☐ Money Order
Please charge my ☐ Visa   ☐ Mastercard
Card # _____ Exp. Date _____
Signature on Card _____
Mail to: Name   _____
Address   _____
               _____
Telephone   _____
       ☐ **With order, send me "Effective Fundraising Tips."**

--- ✂ ---

Please send ___ copies of *"Medley of First Nations Cooking"*
    at $19.95 each $_____

Postage & Handling: $3.00 for 1 book; $1.00 for
    each additional book (not applicable on orders
    of 5 to 10 books) $_____

                           Total enclosed $_____

Enclosed is my ☐ Cheque ☐ Money Order
Please charge my ☐ Visa   ☐ Mastercard
Card # _____ Exp. Date _____
Signature on Card _____
Mail to: Name   _____
Address   _____
               _____
Telephone   _____
       ☐ **With order, send me "Effective Fundraising Tips."**

Service With A Personal Touch

Medley of First Nations Cooking are great gifts for Wedding Showers, Birthdays, Mother's Day, Christmas, etc. We'll ship the books to the recipient of your choice. Include a note or card and we'll be happy to include with order.

Mail to: **First Nations Cooking, Box 292, Deseronto, ON   K0K 1X0**

CONVENIENT ORDER FORMS

For order of 5 to 10 books, we'll pay the shipping to **one** address. We offer attractive discounts on orders of 10 books or more. For details: **613-396-1435**
Email: *spiritalive@sympatico.ca*
Tremendous for Fundraising!

Please send ____ copies of *"Medley of First Nations Cooking"*
   at $19.95 each $_____
Postage & Handling: $3.00 for 1 book; $1.00 for
   each additional book (not applicable on orders
   of 5 to 10 books) $_____
                  Total enclosed $_____
Enclosed is my ☐ Cheque ☐ Money Order
Please charge my ☐ Visa   ☐ Mastercard
   Card # _____ Exp. Date _____
   Signature on Card _____
Mail to: Name   _____
Address   _____
           _____
Telephone   _____
     ☐ **With order, send me "Effective Fundraising Tips."**

✂

Please send ____ copies of *"Medley of First Nations Cooking"*
   at $19.95 each $_____
Postage & Handling: $3.00 for 1 book; $1.00 for
   each additional book (not applicable on orders
   of 5 to 10 books) $_____
                  Total enclosed $_____
Enclosed is my ☐ Cheque ☐ Money Order
Please charge my ☐ Visa   ☐ Mastercard
   Card # _____ Exp. Date _____
   Signature on Card _____
Mail to: Name   _____
Address   _____
           _____
Telephone   _____
     ☐ **With order, send me "Effective Fundraising Tips."**

Service With A Personal Touch

Medley of First Nations Cooking are great gifts for Wedding Showers, Birthdays, Mother's Day, Christmas, etc. We'll ship the books to the recipient of your choice. Include a note or card and we'll be happy to include with order.

Mail to: **First Nations Cooking, Box 292, Deseronto, ON   K0K 1X0**